# Moderating
# Focus Groups

Richard A. Krueger

# Moderating
# Focus Groups

Focus Group Kit**4**

**SAGE Publications**
*International Educational and Professional Publisher*
Thousand Oaks  London  New Delhi

*For information:*

SAGE Publications, Inc.
2455 Teller Road
Thousand Oaks, California 91320
E-mail: order@sagepub.com

SAGE Publications Ltd.
6 Bonhill Street
London EC2A 4PU
United Kingdom

SAGE Publications India Pvt. Ltd.
M-32 Market
Greater Kailash I
New Delhi 110 048 India

Printed in the United States of America

*Library of Congress Cataloging-in-Publication Data*

Morgan, David L., Krueger, Richard A.
    The focus group kit.
        p.    cm.
    Includes bibliographical references and indexes.
    Contents: v. 1. The focus group guidebook/David L. Morgan. v. 2. Planning focus groups/David L. Morgan. v. 3. Developing questions for focus groups/Richard A. Krueger. v. 4. Moderating focus groups/Richard A. Krueger. v. 5. Involving community members in focus groups/Richard A. Krueger, Jean A. King. v. 6. Analyzing and reporting focus group results/Richard A. Krueger.

ISBN 0-7619-0760 (pbk.: The focus group kit: alk. paper)

    1. Focus groups.  I. Title.  II. Series.  III. Morgan, David L.  IV. Krueger, Richard A.

H61.28K778 1997
001.4′33—dc21                                                                                      97-21135

ISBN 0-7619-0818-8 (v. 1 pbk.)
ISBN 0-7619-0817-X (v. 2 pbk.)
ISBN 0-7619-0819-6 (v. 3 pbk.)
ISBN 0-7619-0821-8 (v. 4 pbk.)
ISBN 0-7619-0820-X (v. 5 pbk.)
ISBN 0-7619-0816-1 (v. 6 pbk.)

This book is printed on acid-free paper.

99  00  01  02  03   10  9  8  7  6  5  4

| | |
|---|---|
| *Acquiring Editor:* | Marquita Flemming |
| *Editorial Assistant:* | Frances Borghi |
| *Production Editor:* | Diana E. Axelsen |
| *Production Assistant:* | Karen Wiley |
| *Typesetter/Designer:* | Janelle LeMaster |
| *Cover Designer:* | Ravi Balasuriya |
| *Cover Illustration:* | Anahid Moradkhan |
| *Print Buyer:* | Anna Chin |

# Brief Table
# of Contents

# Detailed Table
# of Contents

# Acknowledgments

I had known David Morgan for a number of years. Over the years we shared an interest in focus groups, and regularly our paths had crossed at professional events, at airports, or electronically by phone and e-mail. I found his advice and counsel on focus group interviewing to be valuable, particularly as academic institutions began to embrace qualitative research procedures.

One day, the phone rang and it was David on the line. He asked if I'd be interested in working with him on a writing project on focus groups. He was vague and the ideas weren't fleshed out, but he got me interested. After weeks of pondering alternatives, we agreed that we'd pool our ideas and attempt to produce a workable kit for researchers. The field of focus group research was changing rather quickly and, as we learned new strategies and concepts, we wanted to pass these along to others.

David insisted that the kit of books had to be complete, but I was more interested in enjoying the journey of writing. The process of writing shouldn't be drudgery but rather provide some enjoyment, perhaps both to the reader and the author. Looking back, it's been a pleasure to work with David on this project. He helped shape the approaches and was generous with his praise, offering insightful and valuable suggestions throughout the process. We both got our wishes. We feel that the information is complete, and we had a reasonable amount of fun in preparing it for you.

Others have been instrumental in this book. Mary Anne Casey read and reread each section and offered enormous help in the logical flow and content of the book. Her enthusiasm, wit, and kindness added greatly. In reality, she is the coauthor, although her name is not listed on the cover. I've been fortunate to retell her stories; often, I've received credit when in fact I was merely repeating her experiences. Dr. Casey has helped teach hundreds of aspiring moderators and she, more than anyone else, reflects the qualities of the best moderators in showing empathy and sensitivity. She brought logic when I didn't know where I was going, she found the right word when I was confused, she added quality to the presentation in too many ways to mention.

I tip my hat to hundreds of veteran focus group moderators throughout the country. I've watched many of them, listened to their stories, and read quite a few of their reports. They are a dedicated group of applied researchers from both academic and others from applied fields. My thanks to those who have taught me so much about focus group interviewing: Carol Bryant, Harold Cook, Mary Debus, Tom Greenbaum, Naomi Henderson, Reyn Kinzey, Ed Nelson, Marilyn Raush, Gail Redd, Ed Virant, and Rhonda Wiley-Jones.

Thanks to my colleagues at the University of Minnesota for fostering a learning environment. I am especially appreciative of the guidance from George Copa, Judy Garrard, Jean King, Caroline Turner, and Howard Williams.

Networks and contacts are critical. The American Evaluation Association and the Qualitative Research Consultants Association provided valuable forums for interaction and collegial sharing.

The production quality was improved by Susan Wladaver-Morgan, who offered helpful editing suggestions. The staff at Sage Publications continually were most helpful. Their editors were encouraging, creative, and willing to take risks. Special thanks to Diana Axelsen, Ravi Balasuriya, Marquita Flemming, and C. Deborah Laughton, for eagerly contributing their talents.

A good book is one that touches us in several ways. It should be serious, yet funny. It should be challenging, yet comfortable. It should raise the level of thought. But most of all, it should be fun to read. The best test is if you read more than what you intended. I hope that this book does that for you. May you find the insight, the seriousness, the guiding principles, and the humor in this volume.

# Introduction to the Focus Group Kit

We welcome you to this series of books on focus group interviewing. We hope that you find this series helpful. In this section we would like to tell you a bit about our past work with focus groups, the factors that led to the creation of this series, and an overview of how the book is organized.

We began our studies of focus group interviewing about the same time. Our academic backgrounds were different (David in sociology and Richard in program evaluation), and yet we were both drawn to focus group interviewing in the 1980s. We both had books published in 1988 on focus group interviewing that resulted from our research and practice with the methodology. At that time, we were unaware of one another's work and were pleased to begin a collegial relationship. Over the years, we've continued our studies independently, and occasionally our paths crossed and we had an opportunity to work together. In the last decade, we've worked together in writing articles, sharing advice on research studies, and teaching classes. We have generally found that we shared many common thoughts and concerns about focus group interviewing.

During the 1990s, we found that interest in focus groups continued, and we both prepared second editions for our 1988 books. In 1995, the staff at Sage Publications asked us to consider developing a more in-depth treatment of focus group interviewing that would allow for more detail and guide researchers beyond the basic issues. We pondered the request and thought about how the materials might be presented. We weighed a variety of options and finally developed the kit in its present form. We developed this kit in an effort to help guide both novices and experts.

In these books, the authors have occasionally chosen to use the word *we*. Although the authors share many common experiences with focus groups, our approaches can and do vary, as we hope is the case with other researchers as well. When you see the word *we* in the books of this series, it typically refers to a judgment decision by the specific author(s) of that particular volume. Much of what the authors have learned about focus groups has been acquired, absorbed, and assimilated from the experiences of others. We use *we* in circumstances where one of us personally has experienced a situation that has been verified by another researcher or when a practice or behavior has become standard accepted practice by a body of focus group moderators. The use of *I,* on the other hand, tends to refer to situations and experiences that one of us has witnessed that may not have been verified by other researchers.

In terms of content, we decided on six volumes, each representing a separate theme. The volumes include the following:

- **Volume 1:** *The Focus Group Guidebook*

This volume provides a general introduction to focus group research. The central topics are the appropriate reasons for using focus groups and what you can expect to accomplish with them. This book is intended to help those who are new to focus groups.

- **Volume 2:** *Planning Focus Groups*

This volume covers the wide range of practical tasks that need to get done in the course of a research project using focus groups. A major topic is making the basic decisions about the group's format, such as the size of the groups, their composition, and the total number of groups.

- **Volume 3:** *Developing Questions for Focus Groups*

This book describes a practical process for identifying powerful themes and then offers an easy-to-understand strategy for translating those themes into questions. This book helps make the process of developing good questions doable by outlining a process and offering lots of examples.

- **Volume 4:** *Moderating Focus Groups*

The book is an overview of critical skills needed by moderators, the various approaches that successful moderators use, and strategies for handling difficult situations. Rookie moderators will find this book to be an invaluable guide, and veteran moderators will discover tips and strategies for honing their skills.

- **Volume 5:** *Involving Community Members in Focus Groups*

This book is intended for those who want to teach others to conduct focus group interviews, particularly nonresearchers in communities. Volunteers can often gather and present results more effectively than professionals. A critical element is how the volunteers are trained and the manner in which they work together.

- **Volume 6:** *Analyzing and Reporting Focus Group Results*

Analysis of focus group data is different from analysis of data collected through other qualitative methodologies and this presents new challenges to researchers. This book offers an overview of important principles guiding focus group research and then suggests a systematic and verifiable analysis strategy.

Early on we struggled with how these materials might be presented. In order to help you find your way around the series, we developed several strategies. First, we are providing an expanded table of contents and an overview of topics at the beginning of each chapter. These elements help the reader quickly grasp the overall picture and understand the relationship between specific sections. Second, we've attempted to make the indexes as useful as possible. Volumes 2-6 contain two indexes: an index for that volume and a series index to find your way around the entire kit of six books. Finally, we are using icons to identify materials of interest. These icons serve several purposes. Some icons help you locate other materials within the series that amplify a particular topic. Other icons expand on a particular point, share a story or tip, or provide background material not included in the text. We like the icons because they have allowed us to expand on certain points without interrupting the flow of the discussion. The icons have also allowed us to incorporate the wisdom of other focus group experts. We hope you find them beneficial. We've also included icons in the book to help you discover points of interest.

The **BACKGROUND** icon identifies the bigger picture and places the current discussion into a broader context.

The **CAUTION** icon highlights an area where you should be careful. These are especially intended to help beginners spot potholes or potential roadblocks.

The **CHECKLIST** icon identifies a list of items that are good to think about; they may or may not be in a sequence.

The **EXAMPLE** icon highlights stories and illustrations of general principles.

The **EXERCISE** icon suggests something you could do to practice and improve your skills, or something you could suggest to others to help them improve their skills.

The **GO TO** icon is a reference to a specific place in this book or one of the other volumes where you will find additional discussion of the topic.

The **KEY POINT** icon identifies the most important things in each section. Readers should pay attention to these when skimming a section for the first time or reviewing it later.

The **TIP** icon highlights a good practice to follow or an approach that has worked successfully for us.

We hope you find this series helpful and interesting.

—Richard A. Krueger
*St. Paul, Minnesota*

—David L. Morgan
*Portland, Oregon*

# 1

# About This Book

"I found it to be a challenge. On the one hand, There are some considerations. It looks so easy." When focus group moderating is done well, it looks very easy. The moderator is relaxed, in control, friendly, having fun, and getting participants to tell all about themselves. Because experts make moderating look so easy, some rookie moderators have been surprised by the complexity and difficulty of the task.

This book is intended to help you inventory your present moderating skills and suggest strategies for how you might fine tune your ability to conduct focus group interviews. "What do I do well? What do I need to improve?" These are questions we hear moderators ask themselves—and unfortunately there is limited opportunity for feedback.

Effective moderating requires a complex set of skills. Each person who attempts to moderate brings richness and uniqueness to the experience. Over the past decade, we have taught hundreds of people to moderate. But, in fact, we've found that often we were students, and the novice moderators taught us new and varied strategies of communication. It is difficult to script exact strategies. There just is not one right way to conduct a successful focus group. We've tried to capture this spirit in this book and found it to be a challenge. On one hand, there are some considerations that are critical (friendliness, a permissive approach, a nonthreatening environment), but individuals show these in a variety of ways. If we overly emphasize the critical components, we foster a rigid attitude. If we overly emphasize the individual approaches, we foster a wishy-washy, anything-goes approach. We've tried to steer a middle course.

We have purposely opted to describe the interviewer's role by using the term *moderator*. This term highlights a specific function of the interviewer—that of moderating or guiding the discussion. The term *interviewer* tends to convey a more limited impression of two-way communication between an interviewer and an interviewee. By contrast, the focus group affords the opportunity for multiple interactions, not only between the interviewer and the respondent but among all participants in the group. The focus group is not a collection of simultaneous individual interviews but rather a group discussion where the conversation flows easily with nurturing by the moderator.

We're sharing ideas and suggestions as we would offer them to a friend—a friend who is about to conduct a focus group. When sharing with friends, our intent is to accomplish the desired results in a pragmatic manner. We offer strategies that we've found to be helpful in conducting focus groups, but we also want you to adapt these strategies based on your personal skills and situation.

An assumption inherent in this book is that you probably won't read the volume from beginning to end. We've found that many researchers regularly skip sections, go back and forth to topics of interest, and skim other chapters. We've tried to organize the book so that you can quickly find your areas of concern and just maybe discover some interesting information that you hadn't anticipated along the way. We would feel successful if you find more than you anticipated in this book.

# 2

# Guiding Principles of Moderating

Overview

*Be Interested in the Participants—*
*Show Positive Regard*
*Be a Moderator, Not a Participant*
*Be Ready to Hear Unpleasant Views*
*You Can't Moderate All Groups*
*Use Your Unique Talents*

## Be Interested in the Participants— Show Positive Regard

Moderator respect for participants is one of the most influential factors affecting the quality of focus group results. The moderator must truly believe that participants have valuable wisdom, no matter what their level of education, experience, or background.

Indeed, participants may have limited knowledge, hold opposing values to those of the researchers, or have seemingly fuzzy logic, but still the moderator listens attentively and with sensitivity.

After moderating three or four focus groups, the moderator will have heard the topic discussed in a variety of ways, and many concerns and key ideas will have been expressed several times. At this point, the information is old stuff to the moderator, but it

KEY POINT

**The Moderator Must Truly Believe That Participants Have Wisdom**

still deserves the respect and active listening that was present the first time it was heard. Lack of respect quickly telegraphs to participants and essentially shuts down meaningful communication. Why should participants share their personal feelings when the moderator is arrogant? The moderator must truly believe that the participants have wisdom and insights that need to be uncovered.

Empathy and positive regard are critical qualities for an effective moderator. The moderator truly believes that those gathered for the discussion have unique wisdom and valuable insights. This attitude must permeate the entire focus group environment. Here's a meditation developed by Jack Kornfield (1993, p. 82) that reflects the spirit of moderating focus groups. We hope that those planning to moderate find it beneficial.

---

**EXERCISE**

**Meditation: Seeing All Beings as Enlightened**

*Picture or imagine that this earth is filled with Buddhas, that every single being you encounter is enlightened, except one—yourself! Imagine that they are all here to teach you. All those you encounter are acting as they do solely for your benefit, to provide just the teachings and difficulties you need to awaken.*

*Sense what lessons they offer to you. Inwardly thank them for this. Throughout a day or a week continue to develop the image of enlightened teachers all around you. Notice how it changes your whole perspective on life.*

—Jack Kornfield

---

One benefit of conducting focus groups is the insight and wisdom that accrue to the moderators. Trevor Collier said it well in *The Secret Life of Moderators*, an address to the 1996 Qualitative Research Consultants Association annual conference in Montreal.

---

**EXAMPLE**

**Be Open to Learning**

*What a lot our respondents give us! For one thing, talking to them in groups, triads and one on ones has taught me to appreciate the language and longings of generations other than mine. I'm delighted by the energy and restless impatience of the nineteen year old roofer with his baseball cap on backwards. I'm delighted by his pseudo-homey hip talk . . . his super cool "at—ti—tude" and—as I get to know him better—moved by his dewy-eyed idealism.*

*Equally, who wouldn't be entranced by the reminiscences of elderly people, or enjoy spending time with a group of middle-aged female chicken pluckers. Women with an earthy, street-smart appreciation of life, who pounce on every possible double entendre. Two hours with them feels like an evening out at the neighborhood bar.*

*Then too I feel this job has also put me personally in touch with the regional variations of our countries. Ten years ago most of the studies I did were around Toronto. Now, thanks to clients who have realized that the heart of Canada does not beat in Skydome, and there is more to America than a trip to Buffalo, most of the time I work in far flung places. It's a revelation to see how topography, climate and local culture have molded the personalities of people in various parts of our continent and shaped their outlooks on life. And in what other kind of job can one share the stories of oil workers in Edmonton or Houston on Tuesday and those of dock hands in Halifax or San Diego on Thursday.*

*But most of all, doing qualitative research allows us to share, by talking to men and women who are different from us, other visions of the world. And further, to better appreciate the subtleties and complexities of both genders. In my own case, when I began moderating I was, more or less, at ease conducting focus groups with women, and felt fine talking with white collar guys "like me." But when it came to talking with a group of tattooed, hard-nosed, longhaired, fifty-beers-a-week drinkers, some of whom had bounced around just this side of the law for years, I was terrified. I felt they would spot me for a fraud.*

*Eventually, I started to relate. I found things in common with the 24 year old from a public housing project who has never had a real job, and the truck driver who has only been getting home on weekends for twenty years now. There is a directness of feeling in men like that which, when it is given voice, is both moving and humbling.*

*I have learned more about women too. I have put myself in their shoes so often that I feel I can better understand the fear of a woman reentering the work force next Monday after spending the past ten years "just raising a family," or of trying to maintain a sense of self worth when those around her are telling her that what she is doing is of little value. Or the creepy feeling she gets walking into a donut shop filled with men. While I can never live a woman's life, I can at least try to explain it to my, mostly male, clients.*

*I can describe the personal growth gifts that I have been given by this job secure in the knowledge that most of you—my colleagues—have been given the same. Despite the cynicism that we occasionally feel when confronted with professional respondents, for the most part those we talk with are decent people who let us freely into their lives. And, in return, we relate fiercely to them.*

*After all, that is why every moderator worth his or her salt feels shock and revulsion when observers, safe behind their one-way mirror, belittle or make fun of the people who show, in two hours of friendly conversation, that they are only guilty of being themselves.*

—Trevor Collier

---

## Be a Moderator, Not a Participant

The moderator role is to guide the discussion and listen to what's said but not to participate, share views, engage in discussion, or shape the outcome of the group interview. It's easy for the moderator to cross the line and get actively involved in the group.

There are degrees of moderator involvement that range from subtle body language to actively sharing opinions and experiences, and even to leading participants to take action. Some moderators wrongly assume that sharing their personal opinions will foster greater sharing among participants. Unfortunately, this tactic tends to cue participants about what's wanted and may limit the range of views expressed. In some situations, it is not only acceptable but desirable for moderators to share factual or demographic information about themselves. This occurs if the group needs assurance that all participants, including the moderator, have critical factors in common. For example, in some studies with physicians or law enforcement personnel, it has been helpful for the moderators to indicate that they also were MDs or certified law enforcement officers. Going beyond these factual statements to comments of opinions or values, however, begins to add risk and can jeopardize the discussion.

## Be Ready to Hear Unpleasant Views

Moderating requires self-discipline. Focus groups have sometimes been jeopardized because novice moderators could not hold back their personal opinions. Internal researchers and others who have a personal commitment to the topic of inquiry need to be particularly careful to suspend their personal views and seek out the perceptions of the group participants. It's hard to listen to people with limited knowledge of your program offer half-truths and criticize things that are near and dear to your heart. Harder yet is to smile and sincerely say "thank you" after they've been critical. Professional focus group moderators have a distinct advantage in this respect because they are emotionally detached from the topic of the study.

## You Can't Moderate All Groups

Participants must feel comfortable with the moderator. They must feel that the moderator is the appropriate person to ask the questions and that their answers can be openly offered and discussed. There are few absolutes about the physical characteristics of the moderator, because much depends on the situation and the past experiences of the participants. This involves more than having participants feel comfortable with the moderator's dress and appearance. Conscious consideration should be given to factors such as gender, language, race, age, socioeconomic characteristics, and technical knowledge. Each of these characteristics, depending on the circumstances, has the potential for inhibiting communication, especially when there is a perceived power differential between the moderator and the participants.

---

*Recently, an AIDS researcher was planning focus group interviews with prostitutes who were also intravenous drug users. The topic was the use of condoms and sterilized needles in AIDS prevention. This situation presented difficulties to researchers, who understood little of the culture or environment of the target audience. The researchers needed to consider who might lead the discussions. The topic was sensitive, and some of the behaviors were illegal. Clearly, the wrong moderator would get little useful information. In this study, considerable attention was placed on who might be able to lead this discussion in a manner that would illicit truthful answers and open discussion. After some reflection, several possibilities emerged, such as training a counselor who is known and trusted by the participants or a drug-using prostitute to moderate the discussions.*

**EXAMPLE**

**Who Should Conduct the Focus Group?**

---

The moderator is not neutral—no matter how hard he or she may try. The moderator is a member of a racial group, an age category, a gender, and any one of these may be the decisive factor that inhibits or fosters openness within the group. A valuable asset of many nonprofit and public institutions is the ability to recruit volunteer moderators who are not researchers but who possess the critical characteristics essential for success. The critical characteristic may be a quality or characteristic such as gender, age, race, and so forth.

**This Is Discussed in Greater Length in Chapter 6**

## Use Your Unique Talents

Over the years, we've had the opportunity to observe hundreds of focus group moderators and provide help in improving their skills. From these experiences, we've learned several lessons. First, there is considerable value in demonstrating moderating skills to aspiring moderators. Just by watching and listening, a novice moderator can learn a number of effective strategies. The second lesson is that each individual brings unique skills and abilities to the moderating experience. Copying the style of another doesn't work if it seems artificial to you. When the moderator is comfortable and natural, participants will feel more relaxed and willing to share.

How do others know that you're interested in what they're saying? How do participants know that you care about the topic and that you place value in what they're saying? Each of us is

**For More Information, See Chapter 6**

unique, and while there are some global strategies (eye contact, smiles, careful listening, reweaving of comments), each moderator will display these in different ways.

Perhaps the best advice is to watch other moderators and, based on what you see, develop strategies that are comfortable to you and effective for your focus groups.

KEY POINT

**Watch Other Moderators and Develop Strategies That Work for You**

# 3

# What You Need to Do
## Before the Focus Group

## Prepare Yourself Mentally

Moderators must be mentally alert and free from distractions, anxieties, or pressures that limit their ability to think quickly. Moderating a group discussion requires concentration and careful listening. Therefore, you should plan your schedule to minimize the risk of unexpected pressures that might limit your ability to concentrate. Moderators must be able to give their full attention to the group.

The moderator should be completely familiar with the questioning route. Typically, key questions will be limited to between two and five questions, with possible subpoints after each question. The moderator will have a list of questions but will use it only as a reminder of upcoming questions. The moderator will clearly know the rationale for each question and also why that question is placed where it is in the discussion. An understanding of all questions is valuable because the sequence of questions is sometimes modified during the interview. Glancing at the questioning route to remember the next question is acceptable, but reading the question (and losing eye contact with the participants) destroys the spontaneous flow of the discussion.

Moderators must be ready to listen and think simultaneously. It is not enough to be an empty vessel, listening and absorbing the comments of participants. Master moderator Judith Langer (1978, pp. 10-11) offers a series of questions that pass through the moderator's mind while the discussion is in process:

- What else do I need to ask to understand this respondent's statement—what it means, why he/she feels that way, etc.?
- Am I hearing everything I need to know to understand the problem and answer the objectives of the research? Is there a question not on the topic guide [questioning route] that I should ask?
- How much time do I have left? Will I be able to cover everything when just one section of the topic guide could take the full two hours?
- What does all this mean anyway? What am I learning about consumer feelings, beliefs, and behavior? What ideas does this suggest about solving the particular marketing problem?
- How do I get beyond the intellectualizing to respondents' real feelings? I want to reach the level of unanalyzed impressions and emotions—what goes through people's minds before it becomes censored. The issue is, "What do you feel?" not "What is your opinion?"

The moderator must have a past-present-future time perspective throughout the discussion. Moderators must remember what has already been discussed, what is currently taking place, what the next topic of discussion will be, and finally, what it all means.

Moderating is difficult because you are not just guiding a discussion, you are involved in a complex process of generating and analyzing data. In one-on-one interviews, the interviewer has the luxury of concentrating attention on one subject, but in the focus group, the number of subjects is increased and the interaction of subjects dramatically multiplies the complexity.

Without doubt, the moderating process is hard work and fatiguing. Because of the mental and emotional discipline required, we won't conduct more than two focus groups on the same day.

### Practice the introduction and questions

*Be clear about the purpose of the study. Be comfortable with the questions. Don't read the questions, but be able to ask them in a conversational manner after quickly glancing at the script.*

**Ways to Prepare Mentally**

### Arrive early

*Plan to arrive early. Often a minimum of 30 minutes is needed if you are familiar with the location, and 60 minutes is needed if you've never been there before.*

### Check your list

*Make a list of what needs to be done and then do as many of these things as possible before the focus group convenes. The list prevents you from being distracted.*

### Quiet time

*Find a quiet place before the group begins. Spend 5 to 10 minutes in reflection, reminding yourself why you are there (to listen and to learn).*

### Pray

*Pray for understanding, knowledge, patience, and wisdom. Pray in a thankful manner that these individuals have chosen to share their wisdom with you.*

### Meditate

*Meditation can occur in many ways and with varying degrees of discipline. The process will relax you and help you focus attention.*

### Visualize the focus group

*Before the focus group begins, think for a few moments about how it might unfold. Think about sequence, options, and potential problems.*

### Don't use alcohol

*Alcohol dulls your ability to moderate a focus group.*

### Be cautious of medications

*Medication may impair your ability to concentrate and/or remember what has been said.*

### Time between focus groups

*Allow enough time between focus groups to "debrief" with the assistant, record your initial observations, and have a brief rest.*

## Assemble the Equipment

When you are on the road doing focus groups, it is critical that you have the right equipment and materials. Consider investing in a carrying case or bag to transport the materials and equipment.

The first essential ingredient is recording equipment, consisting of a cassette tape recorder and remote microphone. We prefer midprice cassette recorders because they provide decent sound quality and yet have a minimum of jacks and buttons. Although broadcast-quality recorders provide superior sound, the disadvantages are complexity and cost. An excessive number of buttons and jacks just causes trouble. When purchasing a tape recorder, we look for durability and ruggedness combined with simplicity. This equipment will be in and out of travel bags and car trunks, and you don't want it to break in the field. Relatively new on the market are the minicassette recorders, which are very small and have longer recording capacity. Unfortunately, they also have small speakers that make listening torture. The standard cassette recorder is still the old faithful. In remote microphones, we prefer the Pressure Zone Microphone style (PZM) because of its profile and remarkably clear sound quality. These microphones usually have a built-in battery and lie flat on the table. They are omnidirectional and highly sensitive, and they provide crisp sound quality.

Once you have the recording equipment, you need to pack the array of needed papers. Bring several sets of the questions and tablets for yourself, the assistant moderator, and the participants (if needed). If you decide to use registration cards, be sure they are packed. Bring name tents. We prefer the blank 5-by-8-inch index cards folded in half lengthwise with participant's first name on both sides. We just print the names on the name tents. Bring sufficient handouts or demonstration materials.

---

CHECKLIST

**What to Bring to the Focus Group**

Get a sturdy nylon bag with a zipper, like a duffel bag, to hold everything you plan to bring to the focus group. We pack the following things:

- ☐ *Cassette tape recorder with cord*
- ☐ *Remote PZM microphone*
- ☐ *Microphone extension cord and electrical extension cord for recorder*
- ☐ *Blank 5-by-8-inch index cards for name tents*
- ☐ *Extra batteries for microphone*
- ☐ *Blank cassette tapes*
- ☐ *Marking pens*
- ☐ *Writing tablets and pens for moderator and assistant*
- ☐ *Copies of the questions*
- ☐ *List of names, addresses, and telephone numbers of participants*
- ☐ *Address, telephone number, and name of contact person at location*
- ☐ *Road maps*
- ☐ *Coloring books and crayons for children*

☐ *Pens or pencils and small tablets for participants*
☐ *Handouts, prototypes, rating forms, etc.*
☐ *Duct tape*
☐ *Masking tape to hang stuff on walls*
☐ *Box of tissues*
☐ *Flip chart (this probably won't fit in your bag!)*

---

*Don't forget to plan for refreshments. For specific suggestions, see Volume 2 of this series,* Planning Focus Groups.

TIP

**Food**

---

*When on the road with focus groups, I always feel more comfortable with a roll of duct tape. It's easy to carry, it's cheap, and it has several practical uses. I use it to hold down electrical extension cords and to keep the microphone cords from disconnecting. Also, this tape can be used to cover up unneeded buttons and jacks on the recorder. In a pinch it can also be used to hold up pages on the flip chart.*

—Richard Krueger

TIP

**Duct Tape**

---

*Nothing sticks like duct tape, so be careful when you remove it. It can tear paint off walls and stick tightly around cords. Be careful when you remove the strip of tape holding extension cords to the floor. Avoid letting the tape curl around the cord, because then it is almost impossible to remove. My strategy for removal is to hold down the cord with my foot and then carefully pull off the tape.*

—Richard Krueger

TIP

**Duct Tape Removal**

---

## Arrange the Room

As soon as you arrive at the focus group location, stop and scan the room. Get connected with it. Feel the temperature, notice the lighting and other visible distractions, look over the tables and chairs, note where electrical outlets are, and listen for background noise. You'll have only minutes to correct problems, and you'll have to decide quickly if you'll need a replacement room. My order of action is this:

1. Decide if the room is suitable
2. Arrange tables (discussion table, refreshment table, registration table)
3. Arrange chairs around discussion table
4. Set up and test recording equipment
5. Set up refreshment table
6. Set up registration table (if necessary)

If at all possible, the discussion table should be set up so that the moderator is facing the door and the assistant moderator, sitting opposite the moderator and slightly back from the table, is closest to the door. In the event that a late arrival, or anyone else for that matter, comes to the door, the assistant can immediately meet the person at the door and guide him or her to the appropriate place.

The registration table should also be placed near the door. The refreshment table is often placed by a wall near the door, and the discussion table is in the center of the room. An alternative is to have the registration table and refreshments placed in an adjoining room to allow for a get-acquainted, small-talk period before the focus group begins.

---

**Testing the Recorder**

*I've found a valuable way of testing recording equipment. After I set up the microphone and recorder, I push the record button and walk around the table. While walking, I introduce myself, tell where I am, what group is attending the focus group, and indicate the date and time. I speak in a normal tone. Then I rewind the tape and play it back. If the sound is clear, I leave the information on the tape as a leader. If tapes get mislabeled or out of order, I can just play the first 10 seconds and find out the necessary details.*

—Richard Krueger

---

---

VOLUME 4

# 4

# What You Need to Do
## During the Focus Group

Overview
*Register Participants*
*Make Small Talk*
*Introduce the Focus Group*
*Ask Questions*
*Anticipate the Flow*
*Control Your Reactions*
*Be Comfortable With the Pause*
*Probe as Needed*
*Listen*
*Summarize the Discussion*
*Get People to Leave*
*Debrief With Assistant Moderator*

## Register Participants

If you need additional information on the focus group participants, you might want to consider a registration process. This procedure is commonly done in market research focus groups to verify that participants meet screening requirements for the focus group.

These registration forms are less frequently used in the public and nonprofit sectors because these organizations may already

Volume 2, *Planning Focus Groups,* Has More Information on Screening Procedures.

have the necessary background information in customer or employee files. If you don't already have the information or if you seek information not currently on file, you might consider the registration form.

There are essentially two purposes for these forms. One is to verify that participants are reasonably representative of those you want in the focus group. The screens that you had set up may not have worked well enough, and this form serves to ensure that the participants fit your requirements. If in the registration process you discover that a person doesn't belong in the focus group, you'll need to decide whether to excuse him or her from the group.

The second purpose is to aid in analysis. Sometimes a factor in the background of a participant helps explain a view. Occasionally there is a pattern that is explained by a demographic characteristic.

Registration forms are relatively short—usually consisting of a single page. The process should be designed so it doesn't take time away from the later focus group discussion, and the forms should be speedy to fill out. These registration forms can contain the following information:

**Chapter 9 Has More Information on Removing Participants**

- *Name:* Usually we ask for the participant's name, but we occasionally leave it off the registration form. This occurs when other questions are perceived as sensitive or if anonymity is needed. If you do decide to leave off the name on the registration form, however, you have lost the opportunity to use this registration information in your analysis of the comments in the focus group. You will not be able to compare or cluster comments according to participant demographic characteristics.
- *Gender:* This category is not essential if you have already asked for participants' names on the registration form. If you do not ask for names on the registration form, gender should be included.
- *Age:* Age can be a sensitive factor and can be queried in several ways to reduce the sensitivity. One of the easiest ways is by asking by decades, that is, "Are you in your 20s, 30s, 40s, 50s?" Another way is to ask the year in which participants were born. Still another way, and often the least desirable, is just to ask participants to indicate their age in the space provided.
- *Educational level:* Educational level can be asked in several ways. Often the easiest way is to ask participants to circle the number of years of formal education they've had from a list of numbers that range from 6 through 18+. Sometimes it is helpful to place the words *high school graduate*

below the number 12 and *college graduate* below the number 16. Another way to ask education level is to use phrases such as the following, for which respondents just check the category that best describes their educational level:

Grade school
Some high school
High school graduate
Some technical or business school
Graduate of technical or business school
Some college
College graduate
Graduate degree
Professional degree

- *Occupation:* Occupation can be difficult to identify because space is limited and categories are often misinterpreted. Perhaps the easiest way is simply to provide a space for occupation. Several problems occur when asking for occupation. For example, some people will list their employer and not their occupation; others may list vague or imprecise titles (engineer, administrative assistant, private business owner).
- *Income:* This is a sensitive category and is best asked in ranges. For example, which range best describes your total income for the past year?

Less than $14,999
$15,000—$24,999
$25,000—$34,999
etc.

- *Marital status:* Be careful when asking for marital status. People are increasingly sensitive about sharing this information, unless there is an obvious reason to do so.
- *Involvement—past usage, experience, involvement, customer status:* One of the more helpful questions relates to the participants level of past usage or experience with the agency, product, or topic of discussion. Do they use the product or service regularly, occasionally, sometimes, or never? In fact, this characteristic may be so important that it becomes a screening criterion for participation in the group.

---

*The reason for asking should be obvious to the respondent. Asking for personal information because of curiosity or because you might be able to use it is not sufficient. Increasingly, people are reluctant to give information about themselves, particularly in areas that the individual feels to be private or sensitive, such as marital status, age, or income. We rarely use registration forms or ask for this type of information.*

**Ask Only for Registration Information That Is Truly Needed**

EXAMPLE

**Focus Group
Registration Form
—Example 1**

*BACKGROUND INFORMATION*

*1. Your name* _____

       *Last*         *First*

*2. Age*

 ( ) *Below 20*

 ( ) *20s*

 ( ) *30s*

 ( ) *40s*

 ( ) *50s*

 ( ) *60s*

 ( ) *70 or over*

*3. Education*

 *Years of formal education (circle the appropriate number)*

 *6  7  8  9  10  11  12  13  14  15  16  17  18  18+*

*4. Customer Category*

 *Which of the following describe you? (Check all that apply)*

 ( ) *Customer of agricultural programs*

 ( ) *Customer of family living programs*

 ( ) *Customer of youth development programs*

 ( ) *Customer of community development programs*

 ( ) *Customer of environmental programs*

 ( ) *Customer of interdisciplinary programs*

 ( ) *Elected official*

 ( ) *Government agency staff*

 ( ) *Extension campus staff*

 ( ) *Extension field staff*

 ( ) *Extension support staff*

BACKGROUND INFORMATION

1. Age. What year were you born? _____

2. Race

   ( )   African American

   ( )   American Indian

   ( )   Asian/Pacific Islander

   ( )   Hispanic/Latino/Chicano

   ( )   White

   ( )   Other

3. Gender

   ( )   Female

   ( )   Male

4. Categories. Which of the following describe you? Check all that apply:

   ( )   Student at a local college

   ( )   Faculty at a local college

   ( )   Self-employed. Describe _____

   ( )   Employed by public or nonprofit agency or organization

   ( )   Employed by private agency or organization

   ( )   Elected official. Describe _____

**EXAMPLE**

**Focus Group
Registration Form
—Example 2**

## Make Small Talk

Small talk is essential just prior to beginning the group discussion, and moderators must be able to talk casually and comfortably about issues of minor importance. When participants arrive for a focus group session, greet them and make them feel comfortable. You may ask participants to fill out a short registration form that asks questions about demographic characteristics, particularly those characteristics you don't want to discuss within the group. The hosting role should be similar to that when you greet guests in your home.

The function of small talk is to create a warm and friendly environment and to put participants at ease. Avoid the key issues to be discussed later in the session. If participants share their opinions before the session, they may be reluctant to repeat the observations in the group. Purposeful small talk avoids the focused issue and instead concentrates on common human experiences such as weather, children, or sports. Avoid controversial topics (religion, politics, or sensitive local issues) and topics that highlight differences within the group (e.g., income, education, political influence, etc.).

Because participants arrive at different times, small talk maintains the warm and friendly environment until enough participants are present to begin the session. In most situations, the small talk period will last only 5 to 10 minutes, but the two-person moderating team should plan the welcoming strategy in advance. Often, one person (either the moderator or assistant moderator) meets the participants at the door and brings them into the social gathering, while the other person on the team visits with the group, hovering near the refreshment table.

During this period, the moderator and assistant are observing participant interaction and noting individuals who tend to dominate the group, are excessively shy, or consider themselves experts. An individual who talks a lot may later dominate the conversation and should be seated at the moderator's side if possible. Then, if necessary, the moderator can turn slightly away from the more forceful individual and look at less talkative participants, thereby giving a nonverbal and diplomatic signal for others to talk. Shy and quiet participants are best placed immediately across from the moderator to facilitate maximum eye contact. The moderator might expect that about 40% of the participants will be eager and open to sharing insights, while another 40% are more introspective and willing to talk if the situation presents itself. The remaining 20% are apprehensive about the experience and rarely share (Kelleher, 1982, pp. 88, 91).

This strategic positioning of participants can be achieved in a comfortable manner. The moderating team will have a list of participants who are expected to attend the discussion and will prepare name tents to place on the table in front of group members. The moderator will casually yet carefully "drop" the name tents around the table in a seemingly random manner. In fact, the moderator quickly checks perceptions with the assistant moderator, then arranges and places the name tents accordingly.

**TIP**

**Observe Participants Before the Focus Group Begins**

## Introduce the Focus Group

The first few moments in a focus group discussion are critical. In a brief time the moderator must create a thoughtful, permissive atmosphere; provide the ground rules; and set the tone of the discussion. Much of the success of group interviewing can be attributed to this 2- to 4-minute introduction. Excessive formality and rigidity can stifle the possibility of dynamic interaction among participants. By contrast, too much informality and humor can cause problems in that participants might not take the discussion seriously. Veteran moderators testify that groups are unpredictable; one group may be exciting and free-flowing while another group may be restrained, cautious, and reserved. Differences between groups should be expected; however, the moderator should introduce the group discussion in a consistent manner.

The recommended pattern for introducing the group discussion consists of the following:

1. Welcome
2. Overview of the topic—why you're here
3. Guidelines or ground rules
4. Opening question

Note the example of a sample introduction.

*Good evening, and welcome to our session tonight. Thank you for taking the time to join our discussion of airplane travel. My name is Mary Anne Casey, and I represent the Happy Traveler Research Agency. Assisting me is Dick Krueger, also from the Happy Traveler Agency. We want to hear how public employees feel about airplane travel. We've invited people who work in different government agencies to share their thoughts and ideas. You were selected because you are all government employees who work here in the metropolitan area, and you have all traveled by air at least four times in the past year. We are particularly interested in your views because you have had lots of experience traveling, and we want to tap into those experiences.*

**EXAMPLE**

**Sample Introduction to Focus Group**

*Today we'll be discussing your thoughts and opinions about airline travel. We basically want to know what you like and what you don't like about flying and what might be done to improve your experiences. There are no wrong answers but rather differing points of view. Please feel free to share your point of view even if it differs from what others have said. Keep in mind that we're just as interested in negative comments as positive comments, and at times the negative comments are the most helpful.*

*Before we begin, let me suggest some things that will make our discussion more productive. Please speak up—only one person should talk at a time. We're tape recording the session because we don't want to miss any of your comments. We'll be on a first-name basis, and in our later reports there will not be any names attached to comments. You may be assured of confidentiality.*

*My role here is to ask questions and listen. I won't be participating in the conversation, but I want you to feel free to talk with one another. I'll be asking about a dozen questions, and I'll be moving the discussion from one question to the next. There is a tendency in these discussions for some people to talk a lot and some people not to say much. But it is important for us to hear from each of you tonight because you have different experiences. So if one of you is sharing a lot, I may ask you to let others talk. And if you aren't saying much, I may ask for your opinion. We've placed name cards on the table in front of you to help us remember each other's names. Let's begin. Let's find out some more about each other by going around the table. Tell us your favorite place you've traveled in the past year and what made it your favorite. Nancy, let's start with you.*

---

The first question is designed to "break the ice" and get each participant to talk. After the participant has once said something, it becomes easier to speak again. In addition, the first question underscores the common characteristics of the participants and the fact that they all have some basis for sharing information. This first question must be the type that can be answered in about 30 seconds, and as a result, the responses will often consist of descriptive information. This first question cannot demand excessive reflection or long-past memories. Also, in this opening question don't ask participants for too much, like their name, where they are from, where they teach, the subjects they teach, and their favorite free-time activity. People will forget what you asked them.

**Chapter 9 Has More Information on Questions at the Beginning of the Focus Group Discussion**

It is risky to ask the participants if they have questions before you proceed with the conversation. People will ask for more information on the sponsor of the study, the purpose, who else you are talking to, what you have found so far, if you really expect this information to do any good, and so on. It may put you on the defensive. Avoid inviting questions at the beginning of the focus group discussion.

Participants may need to be reminded a second time of the value of differing points of view. The introduction provides the first suggestion that all points of view—positive and negative—are needed and wanted. A second reminder is helpful if the moderator senses that participants are simply "echoing" the same concept. After several echoes on the same idea, the moderator might ask, "Does anyone see it differently?" or "Are there any other points of view?"

For years we've told focus group participants about the ground rules for the discussion. Unfortunately, the term *ground rules* sounds excessively formal and can stifle discussion. Instead, consider alternative phrases, such as "Some things that will make our discussion go better," "suggestions that will guide our conversation," or "strategies that will encourage a good discussion." Consider listing the important factors on a flip chart for added emphasis, particularly if you have a group that seems as though it will need more control.

Give thought to further describing the role of the moderator. For example, "I'll be guiding the discussion and asking questions. We will be discussing 12 questions, and I've indicated the themes of the questions on the flip chart. From time to time I'll be moving the discussion from one question to another so that we're able to talk about all of the topics." This comment gives participants a concept of the scope of the discussion and the time demands that require the moderator to move from one question to another.

The challenge to the moderator is to keep this introduction short with easy instructions and a natural flow. Time yourself giving the introduction. If it takes less than 90 seconds, you might think about what you've left out and if the instructions are sufficiently complete. If, however, you take more than 4 minutes, you might consider shortening the presentation. Excessively long introductions (more than 5 minutes) have two major limitations. First, the attention of the participants begins to waver after several minutes, and less will be remembered. Second, long introductions signal participants that you are more interested in talking to them than you are in listening to them. The focus group participants are the center of attention. You want them to relax, feel comfortable, share their views, and not have to worry about lots of rules and protocol. The instructions should make sense, seem fair, and be respectful.

KEY POINT

**Keep Introduction Short With Easy Instructions and a Natural Flow**

CHECKLIST

*WHEN DESCRIBING DISCUSSION GUIDELINES*

*WE ALWAYS INCLUDE*

- ☐ *We're tape recording this discussion*
- ☐ *No names are attached to any report*
- ☐ *Who sponsors the study and why*

*WE USUALLY INCLUDE*

- ☐ *My role as moderator is to guide the discussion*
- ☐ *Feel free to talk to each other*
- ☐ *We'll be done by _____ (scheduled ending time)*
- ☐ *We're on a first-name basis*
- ☐ *There are no wrong answers, only differing points of view*

*WE SOMETIMES INCLUDE*

- ☐ *You don't need to agree with others, but you must listen respectfully as others share their views*
- ☐ *Rules for cellular phones and pagers (if applicable)*
- ☐ *Who can listen to the tapes*
- ☐ *Who sees the report and how the report will be used*

*WE RARELY INCLUDE*

- ☐ *This is strictly a research project and no sales are involved*
- ☐ *Location of the bathrooms*
- ☐ *Help yourself to refreshments (they'll do it anyway)*
- ☐ *Overemphasis on tape recording or confidentiality*

## Ask Questions

For More Informa-
tion, See Volume
3, *Developing
Questions for
Focus Groups*

Several things are worthy of remembering when asking questions. Be thoroughly familiar with your questions. It's not essential to have the questions memorized, but they should be carefully phrased and appropriately sequenced. The focus group is virtually worthless unless the questions are on target. The questions must be asked in a conversational manner. If participants don't understand the question, the moderator needs to switch quickly to a parallel question that has consistent meaning. Furthermore, the moderator should modify the sequence of the questions or even eliminate a question, if it has been answered in previous discussion.

*Humor can be very effective in a focus group. If somebody says something funny, don't be afraid to laugh. Humor can help defuse delicate situations. Often serious subjects are easier to discuss with a dash of levity. Avoid tasteless humor that relates to gender, race, age, religion, politics, or any other serious subject. Also avoid humor that is at someone's expense. If humor comes naturally, use it.*

**TIP**

**Humor Can Be Helpful**

*Back a few years ago, in a focus group on higher education, the participants were a mix of university administrators and local business leaders. About halfway through the discussion, one of the business leaders turned to the moderator and said, "How come there are six people here who represent universities and only three who represent businesses? That seems unbalanced to me." After an awkward pause, the moderator said, "Well, maybe those who planned the sessions figured that they needed only half as many business people because they were twice as smart as those from the university." Everyone had a good laugh, the tension was defused, and the discussion continued in a productive manner.*

*Part of what made this humor work is that it was known to all participants that the moderator was from an academic environment. The humor was self-deprecating, and the response might have been entirely different if it had been said by a member of the business community.*

**EXAMPLE**

**Humor**

## Anticipate the Flow

Group discussions are unpredictable, and the discussion may flow precisely as planned or take leaps and detours. Moderators are advised to anticipate the various directions the discussion may take and be able to recognize beneficial topics of discussion as opposed to dead ends. For example, in focus groups relating to community organizations, I have found that the discussion often led to an evaluation of agency professionals—a topic that was usually not the purpose of the study. In these cases it became helpful to include a comment in the introduction about the scope of the study: "We are more interested in your opinions about programs, building facilities, and activities sponsored by various organizations and less concerned about the people who deliver those services." Often a "mock discussion" with colleagues familiar with the participants will help identify varieties of responses. One hallmark of a skillful moderator is flexibility in modifying the questioning route on the fly while obtaining the needed information.

The moderator should also be alert to questions that segue into sensitive, controversial, or ethically questionable topics. For example, a focus group on preventing teen use of alcohol can result in teens telling about their drinking experiences. Focus groups on making communities safer can result in individuals talking about their personal experiences with domestic violence. Organizational focus groups on morale or working conditions can lead to negative comments about supervisors or coworkers. Sometimes this information is valuable to the researchers, but at other times the information poses an ethical dilemma. By anticipating the possibility of these topics, the moderator can interrupt if necessary and move the discussion back to the areas of concern.

**What to Do When the Discussion Gets Off Track**

*The discussion can get off topic for a variety of reasons, and in most cases all it takes is a reminder from the moderator to get back on subject. The moderator might rephrase the question or summarize what has been said and then ask for any additional views. Sometimes, however, the conversation gets off track because participants give more than what you asked for. Participants go into detail about something that is of concern to them, but it is not what the moderator intended or expected. Occasionally, participants will reveal personal experiences that are awkward and unanticipated. They could involve details about an abusive situation, the use of drugs or alcohol, or revelations about improper or illegal behavior. The moderator must have a clear concept of how much detail is needed and then know when and how to move the discussion back on track. Consider these six steps:*

1. *Anticipate situations*
2. *Know the boundaries*
3. *Communicate the boundaries*
4. *Interrupt when needed*
5. *Refocus the discussion*
6. *Later, help the participant, if needed*

*For example, suppose that you are attempting to identify strategies to prevent alcohol or drug use by teens. In this discussion, it can be anticipated that someone might start sharing personal details, so the moderator should know just how specific the discussion ought to become. In the ground rules, the moderator might communicate these boundaries, be prepared to interrupt participants if they cross the line, and then refocus the discussion on the topic of concern. In some situations, you may want to talk individually with a participant after the group and suggest how to obtain further help for the particular problem or concern.*

# Control Your Reactions

Moderators should be attentive to how they respond to comments from participants—both verbally and nonverbally. Often, these moderator responses are unconscious habits from past social interactions. Self-discipline and practice are needed to overcome habits such as head nodding and short verbal responses.

*Head Nodding.* Some moderators will continually nod their head as comments are being made. Head nodding can be helpful if used sparingly and consciously such as in eliciting additional comments from participants. Unfortunately, it is often an unconscious response that signals agreement and, as a result, tends to elicit additional comments of the same type. Also, avoid the negative head shake with the head going side to side, which signals the participant that the comment is not needed, not wanted, or wrong. As a rule of thumb, beginning moderators should monitor their head-nodding tendencies. Some veteran moderators avoid nodding altogether, while other moderators make it a practice to nod in a consistent manner to all comments, as if to say, "I hear you."

*Short Verbal Responses.* In many of our typical social interactions, we've become conditioned to provide short verbal responses that signal approval or acceptance. Some of these are acceptable within the focus group environment such as "OK," "Yes," or "Uh huh," but others should be avoided if they communicate indications of accuracy or agreement. Responses to avoid include "correct," "that's good," or "excellent," because they imply judgments about the quality of the comment.

Consider neutral and nonthreatening nonverbal reactions that can help you communicate. Hand gestures, smiles, and facial expressions can be helpful to get someone to talk, to continue to talk, to hold back on comments, or to maintain the flow of the discussion. Here are some nonverbal expressions that moderators have used and their intended interpretation. Keep in mind that these are situational and are open to a variety of interpretations. They must be used smoothly and comfortably by the moderator. Watch yourself and others to see how these are naturally done. Invite others to interpret to ensure consistency of meaning.

**Moderator Body
Language**

| Gesture | Interpretation |
| --- | --- |
| Smiling and nodding | A signal of encouragement given to a participant who has been hesitant to speak. |
| Lifting an eyebrow | An indication of interest, possibly surprise, or questioning what was said. This gesture may encourage a participant to continue speaking. |
| Tilting head and lifting eyebrows | Similar to above but slightly more noticeable. |
| Gesturing with open hand from wrist toward participant | An invitation to speak. |
| Gesturing with both open hands, palms up | We've encountered a dilemma; what do we do? |
| Pointing to a participant | It's your turn to speak. |
| Pointing to one person while holding up other hand to another participant | Two people want to speak at once, so the moderator is the traffic cop. First one person talks, then the other. |
| Leaning into the table | I'm interested; tell me more. |
| Leaning back from the table | Go ahead and talk. I'm just listening. |

Aspiring moderators should be encouraged to practice these techniques within their normal social interactions and to become comfortable with "value neutral" gestures and comments. Practice focus group sessions and coaching advice from others can also prove helpful.

## Be Comfortable With the Pause

One essential technique of moderating is the 5-second pause. The 5-second pause is often used after a participant's comment or after a question by the moderator. This short pause often prompts additional points of view or amplifies the previously mentioned comment. There is a tendency among novice moderators to talk too much, to dominate the discussion with questions, and to move too quickly from one topic to another. Often the short pause will elicit additional points of view, especially when coupled with eye contact from the moderator.

One occasion for the pause is just after a question has been asked and no one is responding. The moderator looks first at one participant and then at another to see if someone might attempt an answer. Sometimes, if there is no response, the moderator may ask the question a second time and then pause again. Some questions just require time for reflection before an answer can be offered. The novice mistakes are speed and offering examples prematurely. It is often better simply to wait for a comment. The moderator might even sanction the thought process by saying, "Take a moment and think about the answer. We'll wait until you're ready to respond."

Another time when the pause is effective is after one participant has made a comment and other participants say nothing. The first comment may be dramatic or emotional. In this case, the moderator might pause and then say, "How do others feel about that?" or "Are there any other views?"

It takes practice and confidence to be comfortable with the pause, but lack of pauses can affect the quality of the focus group results. When the moderator encounters silence, it's a mistake to assume that participants don't know the answer or that they cannot answer. Neither may be true. The problem is compounded when the moderator then offers examples that restrict thinking and limit the discussion. Instead, the more effective strategy is to know when to pause, for how long, and then how to end the pause period. Sometimes it's enough to say, "There is no need to rush. I'd like you to think on this for a moment, and then when you're ready, tell us your thoughts." If no comments emerge, then the moderator might ask, "Tell me why there is no answer to the question."

The 5-second pause can be practiced on family, friends, and coworkers with interesting results. Advance practice allows the moderator to become familiar with this technique, so it can be used comfortably in group interviews.

## Probe as Needed

Another essential technique is the probe, the request for additional information. In most conversations and group discussions, there is a tendency for people to make vague comments that could have multiple meanings or to say, "I agree." When this occurs, the probe is an effective technique to elicit additional information. Typically, probing involves such comments as the following:

"Would you explain further?"
"Can you give me an example of what you mean?"
"Would you say more?"
"Is there anything else?"
"Please describe what you mean."
"I don't understand."
"Tell me more about that."
"How does that work?"

It is usually best to use the probe early in the interview to communicate the importance of precision in responses and then to use it sparingly in later discussion. For example, if a participant indicates agreement by saying, "I agree," then the moderator should follow up with "Tell us more" or "What experiences have you had that make you feel that way?" A few probes used in this way underscore the impression that more detailed answers are needed and wanted.

Sometimes the moderator might ask a probe question to the entire group:

"Who else has something?"
"What about the rest of you?"
"I see people nodding their heads; tell me about it."
"We want to hear all the different points of view. Who
    else has something that might be a bit different?"

The probe differs from the follow-up question in that probes are more spontaneous and follow-up questions are predetermined. Follow-up questions also tend to follow the "if-then" style described in Volume 3 of this series, *Developing Questions for Focus Groups*.

Be thoughtful about probing. It can be extremely time-consuming and unnecessary. When used without thought, it can produce mountains of trivia that overwhelm the analyst. When used thoughtfully, however, it can provide critical insights into the participants' points of view.

## Listen

One of the greatest challenges for novice moderators is to make the distinction between people talking and people answering the question. It's dangerous to assume that participants are answering the question that was asked just because they are talking. This problem can develop in several ways. The first speaker may think he or she understands the question and begin to tell a story or use an example that redirects the emphasis of the question. Then other participants respond, not to the moderator's question but to the comments of the previous participant. The discussion shifts quickly off topic, and the moderator must pull it back to the original intent. At other times, the participants may provide irrelevant answers because they don't understand the question. This can occur when the moderator inadvertently places emphasis on the wrong word or the participants key their answers off the wrong word in the question.

An important responsibility of the moderator is to decide when enough has been said on a particular question and when to ask the next one. Several factors enter into this decision, including the type of question, the importance of that question, whether participants still have more to say, whether participants are becoming redundant in their answers, the time remaining in the group, and so on. One factor to guide the moderator is the anticipated time needed for each question.

Some questions are of trivial importance and require only a few minutes of discussion, but others may be central to the study and, thus, worthy of considerable discussion.

**Chapter 8 of**
*Developing*
*Questions for*
*Focus Groups*
**Contains More**
**Information About**
**Time Needed for**
**Questions**

## Summarize the Discussion

The moderator has several options for closing the focus group. Perhaps the most common procedure is simply to thank the group members for participating, provide them with the promised gift or cash, and wish them a safe journey home. A far better alternative is for the assistant moderator (or the moderator) to summarize briefly the main points of view and ask if this perception is accurate. When presenting the brief summary, the researchers should watch the body language of the participants for signs of agreement, hesitation, or confusion. When the 2- to 3-minute summary is completed, the moderator invites comments, amendments, or corrections. This summary is often helpful in the subsequent analysis process. It is the first opportunity the research team has to pull together a summary of the overall group discussion.

An additional tactic for closure is to ask the "final question," as described in Volume 2, *Developing Questions for Focus Groups.* The moderator provides an overview of the study and then asks the participants, "Have we missed anything?" A variation of this strategy is useful if participants are reluctant to talk because of sensitivity about the recording equipment. The variation is to turn off the recording equipment, indicate that the discussion is now completed, thank the participants for their assistance, and then ask, "Do you think we've missed anything in the discussion?" This

**Chapter 4 of**
*Developing*
*Questions for*
*Focus Groups*
**Has More**
**Information on**
**Final Questions**

closure may uncover some avenues of thought that were not anticipated.

Before the participants leave, the moderator might ask if they have any questions. This is of particular importance if someone has asked a question at the beginning and was told to wait until later. Inviting questions can be illuminating and provide insights that can be incorporated into subsequent focus groups. For example, a question about who will use the report or the sponsor of the study might be an indication that these need to be described in greater detail in the introduction. Be prepared to tell participants what they might hear from the sponsor in the future. Will participants receive a copy of the report? Will the report be made public? How can participants be kept up to date on future developments? Questions about the report and the future of the study are often signals that participants are interested in the study or concerned about solution strategies.

Occasionally, potentially harmful or misleading information is shared in a focus group. The moderator and assistant should make note of this information at the time it is shared but may often hold back in making corrections for fear of changing the ground rules and dynamics of the group. After all, you have just told them that there are no wrong answers. How can you now say that something is not only wrong, but harmful as well? The strategy that has worked well is to wait until the end of the focus group and then correct any harmful information.

**Chapter 9 Has More Information About Harmful Information**

## Get People to Leave

When the focus group is over, the participants are thanked and told that they can go home, back to school, back to work, or whatever the case may be. Don't be surprised if people don't immediately leave. An interesting phenomenon of focus groups is that participants may feel they want to linger in the company of others. Perhaps they've bonded with others, learned from others, and desire to continue learning more, or perhaps they just want to discuss the topic or some other area of concern in greater detail. At some point, you as a moderator will experience this problem. It is a nice problem because it should be seen as a compliment to your skill that people take considerable interest in the study. Nevertheless, it is a problem, because the moderator and assistant will need to debrief the session as soon as possible and maintain the research schedule. Lengthy delays before debriefing can erode its quality.

After the focus group has concluded, occasionally a participant will offer additional information to the moderator or the assistant. In some cases, the person might wait until others have left or might make a casual comment as the researchers are packing up their equipment. These comments almost always occur after the tape recorder has been turned off. When you hear these comments, be ready to take notes. I'll often reach for my notepad and quickly take notes as the person is speaking. What goes through my mind is why the person waited until the end of the discussion. Perhaps the participant felt the comment wasn't important enough to say during the group, or perhaps he or she didn't want others in the group to overhear it. If the comment is important to the purpose of the study, I may ask such participants why they chose to wait until after the group to share. The answer they offer may be helpful in revising the questions for future focus groups. If the comment is relevant to the study and the researchers feel that it should be included in the analysis, then it should be identified in the notes as a comment that occurred after the focus group ended.

---

*We recently conducted a focus group in a low-income apartment building. The topic, preventing teen abuse of alcohol and drugs, was discussed by eight single parents. The conversation started slowly, but after a few minutes the parents eagerly shared thoughts and ideas with others. Often heard were comments like "I didn't know that other parents were concerned about this. I thought I was all alone," "We really should have been talking about this a long time ago," or "How come the schools, police, or neighborhood association haven't talked with us about these concerns?" When our questions were answered, the parents were told that we were finished and that they could leave. No one moved! No one said a thing for about 15 seconds—which seemed like an eternity. Finally one parent said, "We don't want to leave." Then another said, "Well, if we leave, can we meet again?" We told them that they were welcome to continue the discussion but that we were finished with our questions. If they wanted to meet again, they could certainly do so.*

**EXAMPLE**

**Leaving the Focus Group**

*＊ ＊ ＊ ＊ ＊*

*A colleague was conducting focus groups with young farmers in northern Minnesota. The focus group was to be held in a small township hall in the middle of nowhere. The moderator was worried because a snowstorm was expected and there was the possibility of blizzard conditions. In the 150-mile drive to the township hall, the roads were getting progressively worse, the wind was picking up, and snow continued to fall. The farmers showed up, most of them a few minutes late. The discussion was lively, and the farmers were not only eager to share their views but sought out advice and suggestions from others. By 9:00 p.m., the questions had been answered, and the moderator told the group that she was finished and they were free to leave. After a short pause the farmers resumed their conversation, seemingly ignoring the moderator. A few minutes later, the moderator again said that they were free to leave, and this time she pulled together her papers and started placing them in her briefcase. After a short pause, one farmer said,*

*"It's OK if you leave. We know you're worried about the weather. We want to stay a little longer and talk some more. We'll lock up the building when we leave." She left the farmers in the township hall. We later wondered if they're still there.*

## Debrief With Assistant Moderator

As soon as participants leave, the moderator and assistant should discuss the focus group. This debriefing can vary from 10 minutes to as long as an hour, depending on the complexity and the interests of the research team.

Don't begin the debriefing until everyone else has left the location. If participants don't leave, then the moderator and assistant should depart for a quiet and private location. Some moderators and assistants prefer to have some quiet time to reflect before they discuss the focus group, whereas others prefer to jump right in and talk immediately after participants leave. Either way works. Use whichever approach is more comfortable to the research team. Just before the debriefing, check the tape recorder to see if it captured the discussion. Just rewind it for about 5 to 10 seconds, push "play," and listen. If you don't hear voices on the tape, check other locations on the tape. If the tape didn't work, then you'll need to allocate time immediately to reconstruct as much of the conversation as you can remember. If you hear voices, you can assume that the tape is OK and then record the debriefing at the end of the focus group discussion. You might make a note to the transcriptionist, if you use one, whether or not this part should be transcribed as well.

**Chapter 5 of**
*Analyzing and*
*Reporting Focus*
*Group Results*
**Has More**
**Discussion on**
**Analysis**

As you debrief, consider responding to these questions:

1. What are the most important themes or ideas discussed?
2. How did these differ from what we expected?
3. How did these differ from what occurred in earlier focus groups?
4. What points need to be included in the report?
5. What quotes should be remembered and possibly included in the report?
6. Were there any unexpected or anticipated findings?
7. Should we do anything differently for the next focus group?

The debriefing is the first opportunity for the moderator and the assistant to compare notes. It's not unusual for each person to hear different things and place importance on different issues.

If the moderator and the assistant disagree, it is a signal that they need to listen to the tape.

---

*I usually debrief onto a separate tape which I bring to each focus group. This "summary tape" contains summary comments from the moderator and assistant for all focus groups. When we're in a hurry, this is all we transcribe. This short transcript is then used as a preliminary basis for conducting the analysis and preparing the report.*

—David Morgan

**Consider Making One Summary Tape**

---

# 5

# Selecting the Moderator

Overview

*Professional Moderator*
*Occasional Moderator–Staff Person*
*Volunteer*

A couple of decades ago, there was no choice in who should moderate the focus group interview—it was the professional moderator. Over the past 20 years, a wider spectrum of people have developed focus group skills. We've had a sizable increase in focus group training opportunities during the past decade. Instructional manuals have been prepared, training sessions offered, and formal courses taught in conducting focus group interviews. All of this has produced greater numbers of people capable of conducting focus group interviews. Some people with virtually no training have conducted successful focus groups because of innate ability or just plain luck. Nevertheless, the odds clearly favor preparation, training, and experience.

You need either money or talent to do focus group interviews. Without either you're dead. With money you can hire people with talent. With talent you can do the groups yourself. Three choices are available: a professional moderator, an occasional moderator, or a volunteer. Let's examine these options.

KEY POINT

**You Need Either Money or Talent to Do Focus Group Interviews**

## Professional Moderator

Professional moderators are found throughout the country, mostly in medium-sized to large cities. Many specialize in consumer products, but more are moving into other areas, such as the service sector, organizational issues, and nonprofit and public sector marketing. Also, professional moderators are tending to specialize in certain areas like pharmaceuticals or financial services, and as a result they are serving as a cross between moderator and consultant. Indeed, some of these moderators know as much about the client's product and operation as the client does.

Professional moderators offer several advantages. They bring experience in working with people. Experience helps one know when to probe, how to get information without leading participants, how to make people feel comfortable, and how to refocus questions and keep the discussion on track. They have a neutrality that is essential for certain studies. They clearly convey a nonbiased atmosphere. Perhaps the finest moment for professionals is in difficult situations when something doesn't go well. The professional has experienced these things before and can deftly change a disaster into a valuable learning experience. In moments like this, professionals are worth their weight in gold. One disadvantage is the "gold" you pay to employ the professional moderator.

BACKGROUND

**The Cost of Focus Groups**

*A rule of thumb suggested by market researchers is that the client should expect to pay $3,000 to $5,000 for each focus group, and sometimes more. This rate includes room rental, honorariums, food, recruiting costs, and so forth. The largest portion of the cost is researcher time for planning, moderating, and analyzing the focus group. In public and nonprofit organizations, these costs can sometimes be reduced by using organizational resources. As you can see, it might take $10,000 to $15,000 to conduct a minimum number of focus group interviews. This is described in more detail in Volume 2 of this series,* Planning Focus Groups. *The going rate for conducting focus group interviews varies somewhat because of moderator experience, difficulty in planning and conceptualizing the study, recruitment needs, and a host of other factors.*

In addition to expense, professional moderators may have other disadvantages. Sometimes, they have limited knowledge of the topic, especially when compared with a staff person or a volunteer who may have years of experience with the organization or topic. Another disadvantage of the professional is that the particular study may need a moderator with unique qualifications to ensure the comfort of other participants. Sometimes, factors such as language, race, gender, age, background, or occupation contribute significantly to the focus group's success or failure.

## Occasional Moderator–Staff Person

An advantage of using staff members as moderators is their familiarity with the organization, its history, and its culture. Often, they can get up to speed on the topic almost immediately, and their rich background can be a valuable grounding for analyzing results. This familiarity, however, can also be a disadvantage in situations where traditions are not examined critically and assumptions are made that limit the study. The continual challenge to internal investigators is to get attuned to the assumptions and limits that they often unconsciously embrace. The first step is to be aware of this potential limitation. This effect can be minimized by developing a team of researchers and drawing on their insights. This team can be composed of a diverse group of internal staff or combined with outside professionals or volunteers.

Another advantage of internal staff is the likelihood that involved staff will use the results. Too often reports seem to sit on the shelf, especially when prepared by an outside consultant. When staff conduct a study, they remember the findings and tend to apply these results in a variety of ways.

At the same time, internal staff may have difficulty in breaking free of routine work responsibilities and being able to dedicate sufficient time to conduct the focus group study. Focus groups take time, and too often there is the assumption that the employee can do this on top of everything else. This is a serious problem and can greatly undercut the quality of the study. Another disadvantage is the time it takes to develop the moderator skills needed to lead the groups. These skills are different from traditional small group discussions and staff meetings usually encountered by the employee. Employees may not have opportunity to use these skills in normal work environments, and therefore special practice and review must take place.

## Volunteer

When we speak of volunteers, we are referring to individuals who are not formally employed by the organization and are not employed as consultants or professional moderators. In some situations, these people might actually receive slight compensation for their efforts, and in most situations they are reimbursed for expenses. These volunteers could represent a variety of different types. Volunteers might be people who have had connections with the agency or organization in the past, those functioning as interns seeking to improve their skills, or individuals dedicated to the cause and offering their time and talent as a contribution.

A central advantage of volunteers is in the potential for diversity and the availability of linkages. In situations when the moderator must be of a certain background, you may be more likely to find such a person from within your volunteer ranks. This can occur, for example, where an organization or community needs someone who speaks Spanish, a female moderator of Cambodian background, a senior citizen, or a physician. Volunteers who have access to people, groups, and organizations are a significant asset. In delicate situations such a person can make contacts with the target audiences and obtain valuable advice on focus group strategies and procedures.

The disadvantage of using volunteers is their need for essential skills that are acquired by training and experience. Clearly, the professional will have more experiences to draw on, but volunteers may have unique credibility and insights on the topic.

# 6

# Personal Qualities of Moderators

**Overview**

*Understanding of Group Process*
*Curiosity*
*Communication Skills*
*Friendliness and a Sense of Humor*
*Interest in People*
*Openness to New Ideas*
*Listening Skills*

When selecting a moderator, it is important to look for certain personal characteristics that have particular relevance to leading a focus group. These attributes have a profound influence on the nature of the group interaction and thereby affect the quality of discussion. Here are some personal characteristics that have been helpful to moderators.

## Understanding of Group Process

The moderator should be comfortable and familiar with group processes. Previous experience in working with groups or training in group dynamics is helpful. Amy Andrews (1977, p. 128) expands on this requirement:

> Since half of the moderator's function is to stimulate and guide the group, a knowledge of group dynamics would seem to be an important criterion for selection. For example, the moderator must know how to deal with a quiet, passive group, an overly exuberant group, an outspoken group member, a group member who is unqualified, a group which consistently goes off on a tangent, a group which appears to be giving inconsistent responses, a group which does not understand the question, a group which misses the point completely, a group which is inarticulate, a hostile group or group member, a nervous, tense group discussing a sensitive subject, etc.

The moderator exercises a mild, unobtrusive control over the group. As the discussion proceeds, irrelevant topics may be introduced by participants, and the moderator carefully and subtly guides the conversation back on target. Part of the skill of moderating is the ability of the moderator to make these transitions and yet maintain group enthusiasm and interest for the topic. The moderator also must have a sense of timing—timing for the mood of the group and the appropriateness of discussion alternatives. The moderator must know when to wrap up the questioning and move on to the next issue, promptly but not prematurely.

## Curiosity

The moderator should possess a curiosity about the topic and the participants. Indifference, apathy, and cynicism are quickly spotted by participants and severely hamper the conversation. Furthermore, curiosity may spur follow-up questions and probes that uncover new avenues or connections that yield fresh insight into the topic of study.

Some successful moderators are able to use naïveté to their advantage by prompting participants to amplify their comments, but if used to excess, this approach can become tiresome and inhibit complicated responses. Naïveté is a two-edged sword. In some circumstances, it elicits considerable new information that may have been assumed, sometimes incorrectly, by the moderator. Furthermore, it can produce eloquent statements that place the topic of discussion into a larger context. Unfortunately, this same tactic can become infuriating to knowledgeable participants who feel the moderator has not yet earned the right to ask questions.

## Communication Skills

The moderator must be able to communicate clearly and precisely, both in writing and orally. Complicated questions reflecting fuzzy thinking are confusing. Sometimes, in an effort to be helpful, the moderator asks a question in several ways. The moderator may assume that this strategy helps the participant, but, in fact, it can do just the opposite. If the questions are perceived as different from each other, then the respondent becomes confused about the intent of the inquiry.

## Friendliness and a Sense of Humor

A friendly manner and a sense of humor are valuable assets. Just a smile from the moderator can have considerable benefits. Smiles typically connote warmth, caring, and empathy, and as such they are helpful in promoting conversation. Humor is a powerful bonding agent, particularly when it is spontaneous and not at anyone's expense. Excessive efforts at humor can fall flat, can be misinterpreted, and can be counterproductive. However, if someone says something funny, don't hold back your laugh.

## Interest in People

Talented moderators are truly interested in people. They prefer people over things. They are friendly and like being around people. By contrast, some people really prefer being around technology, animals, the outdoors, or anything but people. The focus group is a social experience, and effective moderators are interested in people—just because they are people.

This interest in people grows out of a respect for each person. Each individual has unique wisdom and insights that are of benefit in the study. The moderator's responsibility is to learn from the wisdom of others.

## Openness to New Ideas

Effective moderators are committed to multiple realities. Although they may have a preference about how something is done, they are open to other methods, approaches, and ideas. When they hear about a way of solving a problem, they don't bring closure but remain open to additional suggestions and strategies.

## Listening Skills

A slight dose of introversion is often helpful to moderators. Moderators who like to perform in front of people, who like to dominate conversations and be the center of attention, must use considerable restraint in the focus group interview. The moderator's role is not to entertain or to tantalize people with wit and wisdom but rather to let participants themselves have center stage. We're sometimes hesitant of those who volunteer to moderate because they feel they are effective in guiding group discussions. Too often these individuals are excessively controlling, presenting views to which others merely acquiesce, instead of allowing participants to generate their own ideas. The better moderator candidates are often those who are reluctant and say, "Who me? I'm not good at speaking in front of groups." We tell them, "That's exactly the kind of person we want! We don't want someone who speaks but, rather, someone who is a good listener." When seeking out moderators, consider looking for those who are capable of careful listening.

# Roles of Moderators

Occasionally, the moderator will choose to take on a specific role in the focus group interview. This role or style is selected because it creates an ambience that influences how participants share information. Moderators often have a preferred style, and it is unknown how successfully we can shift from our preferred role to another assumed role. It has been our observation that those who are successful with a particular role should generally stay consistent within that role. Our guiding principle for beginning moderators is to build on your existing strengths. The main roles are discussed here.

### Seeker of Wisdom

This moderator is out to obtain understanding, insight, and wisdom. This moderator assumes that the participants have that wisdom, and that, if asked the right questions, they will share it. This moderator may have considerable knowledge or expertise in the topic of discussion.

### Enlightened Novice

This moderator is bright but lacks knowledge (or gives the impression of lacking knowledge) in the area of expertise possessed by the participants. The strategy is to get participants to explain more about the topic and causes. Caution is needed with knowledgeable participants, who may be insulted by the apparently uninformed questions of an enlightened novice. (A variation on the enlightened novice is the dumb novice, a role that is not recommended. This moderator has done no homework, does not understand the topic or the participants, and is often just considered to be dumb. As a result, the focus group experience is an insult to participants.)

### Expert Consultant

This moderator is clearly an expert on the topic of discussion and functions as a consultant to the client. A client seeks out such moderators not just because of their ability to lead the focus group but also because they are truly experts on the subject of study. They have worked closely with the client and have learned to think like the client by anticipating concerns and questions. This role is regularly used in the market research sector with consumer products.

### Challenger

This moderator challenges participants to explain, amplify, and justify their ideas and actions. Occasionally, this moderator will even position one participant against another participant who seems to have an opposite view. Challengers need good timing and effective group skills to avoid alienating the participants. Successful challengers can sometimes bring to the surface opposing points of view that may remain undisclosed with other strategies.

## Referee

The referee role provides balance within the group when there are opposing points of view. In a number of situations, moderators quickly assume this role when they discover the group has become polarized. The referee gets both sides to describe their views in detail and ensures fairness and respect for all participants. The guiding principle is fair play. Each person deserves an opportunity to talk but is also expected to listen and respond to the opinions and views of others.

## Writer (AKA the Paper Hanger)

The writer spends a considerable amount of time standing up and writing on a flip chart. Questions are written on the top of the page, and the writer records the comments for all to see. When the page is filled, the writer tears it off and tapes it on the wall for later review. This strategy has several advantages. Participants see what is being recorded and can focus their attention on the specific question at hand. This approach also allows for seemingly immediate correction. The disadvantages are that this moderator-writer needs to stand (a superior position, creating a leader-type role) and that participants need to wait, or feel they need to wait, for the moderator to finish writing before contributing additional thoughts. As a result, this discussion can lack some of the spontaneity and synergy that characterize other moderator strategies.

## Team Member—Discussion Leader Supported by Technical Expert

In this situation, the moderator serves as a discussion leader but is assisted by another team member—one who has a differing area of expertise but who works well with the leader. The moderator guides the group discussion and is assisted by a technical expert who is able to answer complex technical questions in a nonbiased manner. The technical assistant can sit at the table, often opposite the moderator or slightly back from the circle. The technical assistant may also carry out many of the functions of the assistant, described earlier in this book.

## Therapist

The therapist seeks information on psychological motivation or why we think the way we do. This moderator will press participants on some aspects of their behavior or past actions by asking follow-up questions such as "Why is that?" or "Why did you do that?" or "How did you feel?" Participants' comments that may go unnoticed or ignored by other moderators are seized by the therapist as a clue to greater insight and understanding.

## Serial Interviewer

The serial interviewer forgets that this is a group discussion. All comments are directed to the moderator—and in this case he or she is not really a moderator but an interviewer. The participants can sometimes build on other comments, but they are requested to speak directly to the interviewer. As a result, much spontaneity is lost. Although this style is very time efficient, it may miss some critical areas of concern, and it seldom produces much depth or detail.

# 8

# Problems Encountered by Moderators

**Overview**

*Distractions*
*Too Few or Too Many Participants*
*Equipment*
*Room*

There's a game that parents sometimes play with their children. It's a version of "let's pretend" whereby the parent asks the child what he or she would do if certain events occurred. "Suppose that you were home alone and a stranger came to the door. What would you do?" "Suppose that Mom fell and was unconscious. What would you do?" By thinking about possible responses, the child learns options to guide behavior for future events. The child also learns principles that might apply in new situations when there are variations of the rules. In much the same way, there are a number of rather predictable problems that occur in focus groups. By thinking about these events and anticipating responses, the moderator can act quickly and with greater confidence. In this chapter we will review some of these problems.

KEY POINT

**Anticipate Problems That Might Occur in Focus Groups**

## Distractions

A distraction is anything that diverts attention from the topic. Some distractions are major and relate to the meeting room. For example, background music can make it difficult to concentrate and impossible to tape record. Some rooms have visual distractions, such as large windows looking out onto sidewalks or highways. Anything moving can be a distraction. As a result, one of the first tasks for the moderator is to turn off background music and pull blinds or shades to avoid distraction.

Other factors can distract participants as well. Often overlooked are moderator habits and dress. The moderator should be dressed appropriately for the focus group. Being excessively overdressed or underdressed can draw attention. More frequent distractions are extravagant or expensive jewelry. Expensive watches, large diamond rings, and flashy earrings are just fine for many events but should be left at home during the focus group. The guiding principle is that nothing about the moderator should draw attention away from the questions. The smells (perfume, aftershave, hygiene), sights (clothing, jewelry), and sounds (voice) of the moderator should not distract participants.

CHECKLIST

**What to Do When a Medical Emergency Occurs During a Focus Group**

*This will probably never happen to you, but just in case, here are some helpful hints offered by a professional moderator who experienced a medical emergency during a focus group. Suzette de Voggelaere (1995, p. 25) offers the following suggestions:*

- ☐ *Remain calm. Note that all of the following will happen in under five minutes.*
- ☐ *Ask the participant nearest the door to have the hostess\* call 911.*
- ☐ *Check on the participant. Look for a medical bracelet with identifying emergency information.*
- ☐ *Ask the other participants to take their belongings and go to the waiting room.*
- ☐ *Have the facility turn off the tape.*
- ☐ *Call the home number to ascertain whether the participant has any medical history or is on medication. Tell the person answering the phone that because the participant is not feeling well, 911 has been called and the information is needed to give to the medics. Tell the family member that he or she will be called back as soon as the paramedics arrive.*
- ☐ *Discuss/recommend to the client that the group be canceled.*
- ☐ *Ask the clients to leave the viewing room lest they become voyeurs. When the paramedics arrive, they will start working on the patient in the focus group room.*

☐ *Pay the participants. They might ask if they can call the next day to find out how the ill person is doing.*

☐ *In the case of a death, have the facility donate the participant's co-op fee (honorarium) (up to $50, $75, etc.) to the American Heart Association, per the family's request or whatever seems appropriate under the circumstances.*

☐ *Once the paramedics have left, check the focus group room for any signs of activity, such as blood and bodily fluids. The facility may need to have the carpet and the room professionally cleaned and sterilized.*

*\*Market research focus group facilities have individuals called hostesses who are responsible for food, welcoming participants, registration procedures, etc.*

---

*Cellular phones and pagers can be enormously distracting for all participants in a focus group. Not only does the sound distract, but you usually lose a participant—for a few minutes, if you're lucky, and potentially for the remainder of the focus group. Here's a suggestion on how to handle this growing problem. If you see participants bringing cellular phones and pagers into the focus group, add another ground rule. It might be something like this: "This discussion will last two hours. I've noticed that several of you have cellular phones or pagers, and these may be distracting to our discussion. If at all possible, I would like you to turn these off during our discussion. If this is not possible, please leave the room to respond to your phone or pager, and return as quickly as you can. If it's an emergency and you need to leave, please let us know."*

**Cellular Phones and Pagers**

---

## Too Few or Too Many Participants

The problems with participants usually falls into one of two categories: not enough or too many. Let's take these problems one at a time.

### Too Few Participants

It's time for the focus group to begin, but only three people are present. What should you do?

Usually moderators will wait just a few more minutes (perhaps 10 minutes beyond when the group was to start) and then begin. The assistant moderator can meet latecomers as they arrive and give them a quick briefing on what has previously been discussed. In some groups of people, lateness is the norm. If that's the case, then the moderator will need to allow more time for introductory activities. At other times, there may be a special activity or event that conflicts and should be avoided in the future.

Review the entire invitation protocol. Ask those who do show up how they were invited. Did participants receive sufficient notification? (Note the "Background" discussion on systematic notification procedure on page 53.) Was the invitation personalized by sending individual letters out to each participant? Did invitations arrive in a timely manner? Was the incentive sufficient? Any of these variables can dramatically influence attendance.

Some moderators have resorted to overrecruiting as a way to solve the problem of limited attendance, but we recommend against using this procedure. Overrecruiting ignores the problem that is occurring. The challenge is to spot the problem and correct it. As a result of receiving personalized invitations and appropriate incentives, people should want to attend. Just inviting more people can cause additional problems, such as what to do with too many participants. We have found that with careful attention to recruiting and incentives, we regularly get more than 90% attendance.

CHECKLIST

**Diagnose Your Attendance Problems**

*When people don't show up for the focus group, we start asking a number of questions—of ourselves, of those who may have assisted us with recruitment, of those who did show up, and of those who were invited but didn't attend. Here are the questions that we ask:*

☐ *Did participants actually receive phone calls and letters of invitation?*
☐ *Did we avoid conflicts in scheduling the focus groups?*
☐ *Did our invitations convey sincerity?*
☐ *Were participants told why the topic was important to them?*
☐ *Did we convey that their opinions would be valued?*
☐ *Did the recruiter get a commitment from the participant to attend?*
☐ *Did we send several reminders? (systematic notification procedure)*
☐ *Were the reminders personalized?*
☐ *Did we describe the incentive?*
☐ *Was our incentive appropriate?*
☐ *Was our incentive sufficient?*
☐ *Was the location appropriate?*

*Systematic notification procedures seek to ensure that those who were invited to the focus group actually attend. The procedures include the following:*

1. *Establishing meeting times for the group interviews that don't conflict with existing community activities or functions.*
2. *Inviting participants via telephone (or in person) approximately 10 to 14 days before the focus group session.*
3. *Sending a personalized invitation just after the telephone or in-person invitation.*
4. *Telephoning all potential participants the day before the focus group, reminding them of the session and inquiring about their intention to attend.*

BACKGROUND

**Systematic Notification Procedure**

### Too Many Participants

A different problem is having too many people show up for the focus group. Although this might sound like a delightful situation, it really does present problems. Too many people can ruin the focus group, and the wrong people can bias the results.

Sometimes, too many people show up for the focus group when the researcher or moderator gives away control of the recruitment. This occurs occasionally in public and nonprofit environments when someone from the sponsoring organization takes responsibility for recruiting. We've learned to be extraordinarily precise in our instructions, because these volunteer recruiters may take liberties that greatly influence focus group quality. In one situation, a local organization had assembled more than 30 people for the focus group, and the research team was unaware of this until they arrived at the location.

Some situations are rather predictable and can be anticipated. When conducting focus groups with parents of young children, the moderator might anticipate that some will bring children to the focus group. In these cases the researchers might either offer child care or inform parents that there is no child care but that they will be reimbursed a certain amount for child care, if needed. Young children running in the room or babies crying can completely upstage the discussion, at least from the moderator's perspective. At times, the assistant moderator might function as a baby-sitter and take children into another room. Puzzles, crayons, and coloring books may provide some temporary relief, but not for the entire 2-hour discussion.

Another source of unexpected visitors are those who accompany the invited participants. It could be a spouse, a family member, or a friend who has provided transportation. Quick thinking and diplomacy may be needed to preserve the quality of the focus group. The first rule of thumb is not to let such visitors determine what they will do or where they will sit. Seek out those who don't belong in the group and chat with them in the focus group pre-session. Then make a decision. Some visitors may be allowed to sit in the room, away from the discussion table and often at the back or side of the room. Other times, they are invited to wait in the lounge or another place while the focus group is taking place. At times we've asked visitors to participate in the discussion.

A different category of uninvited participants consists of those who are likely to jeopardize the study. Several categories are possible, including people in positions of authority who need to make decisions about the topic, members of interest groups, and members of the press. All of these individuals are likely to be curious about the discussion and will want to slip in and watch from the side. Be definite, be confident, and be firm as you tell the interested parties that your procedures do not allow for visitors in the discussion area. If you allow them to stay, then you no longer have a focus group interview. You could, however, offer to visit with these individuals following the focus group and share general themes that were discussed.

**Options for When Too Many People Show Up**

☐ *Thank them for their interest but indicate that your research procedures limit the size of the group to eight participants. Alternatively, thank them and indicate that research procedures do not permit others not on the research team to observe the discussion.*

☐ *Thank them for their interest and give them a list of the focus group questions. Ask them to answer these in writing in the next room or to take them home and mail the answers back.*

☐ *Randomly divide a larger group into smaller groups. Pick one group as your target focus group where the moderator and assistant place their attention. In the remaining groups, appoint one person to ask questions and another to record responses. When the discussion is finished, the recorder is asked to leave a copy of the results with the researchers. Ask for the recorder's name and telephone number. After the focus group, quickly review these comments for any differences from the target research group. If something important emerges that is central to the study, call the recorder for additional information.*

☐ *If the assistant has experience in moderating, and if note taking is not critical, you could each moderate a focus group.*

☐ *If one person drove another to the group, indicate when the discussion will conclude and tell the driver where to wait. Often, waiting in another room or lobby is best, although in some cases it may be permissible to have drivers wait in the back of the room.*

*When the objectives of the research demand depth of response from either consumers or business executives, we encourage our clients to recruit six to eight participants rather than the conventional ten. We have also found the smaller groups to be perfect with children and teens, because the session seems less like a classroom and permits the moderator to focus more attention to individuals in the group. (Mariampolski, 1991, p. 42)*

—Hy Mariampolski

**Size of the Focus Group**

## Equipment

Problems with equipment occur regularly. One of the first problems is that something is forgotten or left behind. Some moderators have a designated box or bag that is used exclusively for focus group interviews. They may even have a list of what's included for quick review and inventory.

Perhaps the majority of equipment problems are caused by humans. We've learned to prefer simple cassette recorders because the complexity of sophisticated equipment has a greater potential for error. Using equipment with too many buttons, switches, and jacks is just asking for trouble. Get familiar with your equipment. Test it before going into the field. Here are some of the vexing problems we've had with equipment:

- The moderator forgets to turn on the recorder.
- Something gets unplugged (microphone, tape recorder).
- The assistant doesn't know how to eject the tape and turn it over.
- The play button is pushed but not the record button.
- The microphone is plugged into the earphone jack.
- The microphone battery is dead.

*When you're on the road doing several focus groups at a time, consider using a box to keep your cassette tapes organized. Without a special container, your tapes will get lost in the bottom of the bag, and there's the additional danger of recording over an existing tape. We try to purchase tapes that come in a small cardboard box and then use the box as storage.*

**Use a Box to Store Your Tapes**

**Another Use
of Duct Tape**

*Duct tape has many uses. I've learned to use duct tape to cover up any unneeded jacks on my cassette recorder. For example, I now cover up the earphone jack. I used to keep plugging the microphone into the earphone jack, and, naturally, nothing was recorded! I also place duct tape over any switches or buttons that I won't be needing. It looks ugly on the recorder, but it has saved several focus groups.*

—Richard Krueger

## Room

A great advantage of market research focus group rooms (with one-way mirrors) is that they offer predictably good lighting, comfort, and sound quality. Unfortunately, these rooms are often not conve-nient or affordable for many in the public and non-profit sectors. When you select your room for focus groups, try, if at all possible, to visit the location before the focus group. If this is impractical because of the distance, attempt to contact a colleague or friend who can scout out the location for you.

Be cautious about large rooms, especially those with high ceilings. The room should have sufficient lighting, comfortable temperatures, limited sound distractions, comfortable chairs, and a table or several tables arranged so that people can see each other. Avoid large conference tables because they are so impersonal.

Attempt to find a location that is easy to find and perhaps familiar to the participants. A private room in a popular, local restaurant has potential. Many motels and hotels rent out con-ference rooms or meeting suites at a reasonable cost. Libraries, schools, government offices, and other public locations are also possibilities.

# 9

# People Problems

Overview

*Participant Behavior*
*Participant Comments*
*Participant Questions*
*Removing Participants From Focus Groups*

W hat makes moderating so interesting is the people. Each
focus group is new and unlike the one before. Moderators
will encounter a variety of situations that are brought about by
the participants—something they do, something they ask, or
something they want. Failure to respond can jeopardize the
discussion, and making the wrong response can limit the results
of the focus group. Here are some of the people problems we've
encountered.

## Participant Behavior

One exciting aspect of focus group discussions is that they bring
together a variety of people with differing backgrounds and
characteristics. Sometimes, however, individual characteristics
can present special problems for the moderator.

In our experiences with focus group interviews, we've met
six types of participants who exhibit behaviors that can be a

challenge in focus groups. Each of these may require attention and action by the moderator.

- Experts and influentials
- Dominant talkers
- Disruptive participants
- Ramblers and wanderers
- Quiet and shy participants
- Inattentive participants

### Experts and Influentials

Experts can add great value or present serious problems within a focus group. What they say and how they say it can inhibit others in the group. Participants often defer to those who are perceived to have more education, experience, affluence, or political and social influence. Certain people consider themselves experts because they have had considerable experience with the topic under discussion, because they hold positions of influence in the community, or because they have previously participated in this type of session. One strategy is to acknowledge their expertise and ask to hear from others. "Ben, it sounds like you've had a lot of experience with this. Now I'd like to hear what others think about it. Who else would like to share?"

Another way of handling experts is to underscore the fact that everyone is an expert and that all participants have important perceptions that need to be expressed. For example, "Thank you. Who else has something to share? We're interested in all points of view." In addition, the introductory question should avoid soliciting responses that would identify participants' levels of education, affluence, or social and political influence.

Experts and influentials are familiar with control. If they're not in control themselves, they often expect others to exercise control. In addition, they sometimes become anxious when they sense that a group is not in "proper" control. Some focus group techniques like the moderator pause can be misinterpreted by experts as a control failure, and they may step in and attempt to move the conversation along.

See Chapter 4 of *Developing Questions for Focus Groups* for a Discussion of Introductory Questions

### Dominant Talkers

Dominant talkers sometimes consider themselves to be experts, but much of the time they are unaware of how they are perceived by others. Often, dominant talkers can be spotted in pre-session small talk. As suggested earlier in this book, attempt to seat the dominant individual beside the moderator in order to exercise control by the use of body language. When this strategy doesn't work, then the more frontal tactic of shifting attention verbally is required. For example, "Thank you, John. Are there others who wish to comment on the question?" or "Does anyone feel differently?" or "That's one point of view. Does anyone have another point of view?" Nonverbal techniques also can be used, such as avoiding eye contact with the talker and appearing bored with the comments. It is most important, however, to be tactful and kind, because harsh and critical comments may curtail spontaneity from others in the group.

---

**Learn How to Interrupt Diplomatically**

*If you wait for everyone to finish speaking, there's a good chance that you won't get through your questions. In most focus groups, the moderator must occasionally take charge and move the discussion off of trivial topics to those areas central to the study. This takes the skill of diplomatic interruption. Anyone can interrupt, but this action may be seen as rude, inconsiderate, and disruptive. Doing it poorly can influence later discussion. Therefore, consider these strategies:*

- *Once you've decided that you need to interrupt, start listening to the breathing of the speaker. Don't listen for the words, just listen for the inhale. Find the pattern of breathing. Anticipate when the next inhale will occur and get ready to interrupt. Remember that a person cannot speak while inhaling, so you must act quickly. You might phrase the interruption like this: "Thank you, John. That's been helpful. Let's hear from others in the group," or "That's helpful. Let's move on to the next topic. Perhaps we can go around the table and hear from each person," or "Thank you, we've heard quite a bit about that aspect. Now I'd like to hear about other points of view." Another approach runs like this: "This is a great discussion, but we need to move on."*

- *Don't interrupt in the middle of a story. Stories can be vexing because they are sometimes long, redundant, and unrelated to the issue at hand. Nevertheless, it is often considered rude to interrupt in the middle of a story. About all you can do is to anticipate irrelevant stories. There is a tendency for people who tell one pointless story to do it again.*

- *Don't interrupt when emotions are high. Sometimes, a participant will get off on a crusade with great passion. At other times, a participant might relate an emotional experience that is off topic. Be hesitant to interrupt in such situations because this can be interpreted as ignoring or dismissing something very important to that participant. Usually let the situation defuse by itself and then move the discussion back on topic.*

- *There are differences in our willingness and experience in interrupting. Our traditions, culture, and gender influence our behavior. Get to know the group you are moderating. How accepting are they of interruptions? I've been in some groups where everyone was constantly interrupting. In these groups, it's almost impossible for anyone to finish a thought. In other groups, each person finishes speaking before another speaks. Just by listening and observing your target audience outside of the focus group, you'll get a feel for how and when interruptions might be handled.*

**What to Do When
Participants
Interrupt
Each Other**

*Sometimes people will interrupt each other in the focus group. What should the moderator do? Our advice is to use your judgment based on the level of formality needed for your group. Sometimes you might just let these interruptions occur, if they are spread equally around the group, if the group seems comfortable with these friendly interruptions, and if you have time to let the interrupted speaker talk later. In other circumstances, however, the moderator should take more control to ensure that everyone has adequate time to speak. Think of your moderating role as being like a traffic cop. Your task may be to keep track of who's talking and who gets to talk next. If someone jumps ahead, then the moderator maintains the order. For example, "John, please wait with your comment until Jean is finished talking."*

### Disruptive Participants

Occasionally in a focus group, we will meet someone who exhibits behaviors that are disruptive for other participants. This type of individual can be antagonistic, opinionated, intolerant, and disrespectful of others. In the worst case, these individuals sometimes are incapable of following the rules that guide the focus group, such as "Be tolerant of other views, allow others to speak and listen to what they say. We do not ask that you agree with others, but we do ask that you allow them to share their views." These disruptive individuals will repeatedly interrupt others and prevent the free flow of ideas and opinions. Disruptive participants are regularly driven by a philosophical, religious, racist, or political agenda that considers certain views and values to be superior to others.

Often the first course of action for the moderator is to remind disruptive participants that all views are welcome and that the intent of this gathering is to allow everyone to share their views. "We're not asking people to agree with each other but to listen to the views of others." If the disruptive participant is not able to control himself or herself and to show respect for other views, the moderator will need to remove the offending participant.

**Note the Section
on Removing
Participants From
Focus Groups,
Pages 66-68**

**When You Feel
You've Lost
Control of a Group**

*We're going to take a five-minute break—you can use the restroom or have additional refreshments. When you come back take a new seat. (This is a shift in the room vibes—an altered state.)*

—Luke Henderson

## Ramblers and Wanderers

Rambling respondents use a lot of words and never get to the point—if they have a point. These individuals are comfortable with talking and seem to feel an obligation to say something. Unfortunately, the rambling respondent can drone on and on, eating up precious discussion time. As a rule of thumb, we usually discontinue eye contact with a rambler after about 20 or 30 seconds. The assistant moderator should do likewise. Look at your papers, look at the other participants, turn your body away from the speaker, look bored, look at your watch, but don't look at the rambler. As soon as the rambler stops or pauses, the moderator should be ready to fire away with the next question or repeat the current question being discussed. In the remainder of the discussion, the moderating team should limit eye contact with the rambling participant. The response to the rambler is similar to that for experts, dominants, and disruptives: Look away, don't take notes, and interrupt when necessary.

## Quiet and Shy Respondents

Shy respondents tend to say little and speak with soft voices. It seems that these participants think first and then speak. Others may think and speak at the same time: "I don't know what I think until I say it." These reluctant participants often have much to share, but extra effort is required to get them to elaborate their views and to feel that their comments are wanted and appreciated. If possible, the moderator should place shy respondents directly across the table to maximize eye contact. Eye contact often provides encouragement to speak, and, if all else fails, the moderator can call on a shy participant by name. "Sara, you haven't had a chance to say anything about this. What do you think?" or "Sara, I don't want to miss what you have to say. Would you like to add something?"

## Inattentive Participants

The inattentive participant has difficulty staying on topic. This person is sometimes similar to the rambler in that the answers are off target, but the inattentive participant doesn't seem to hear or understand the question. Answers do not connect with the questions, and the individual may seem preoccupied. While the rambler might know where he or she is going, the inattentive participant forgets or never knew. Anxiety, stress, medication, or preoccupation can all contribute to inattention.

A strategy that may work for this participant is to call the person by name, repeat the question, and ask if he or she would like to say something about it. Although it is impractical to do this for every question, it can be done on key questions. Occasionally, the moderator may interject, "Excuse me, but what we are most interested in is . . ." Another strategy is to write the questions on the flip chart for all to see and remember. This is usually done in advance with one question per page to avoid the participants skipping ahead.

**TIP**

**How to Keep Respondents Under Control**

*Judith Langer (1991, pp. 34-38) offers several suggestions on how to keep respondents from taking over focus groups.*

- *Use hands as if conducting an orchestra. The hands up in a stop pose signals [participants] that they should wind up their comments.*

- *Avoid eye contact. Ignore the respondent.*

- *Say, "Excuse me" or "Sorry, I can't hear you" when several are talking at the same time.*

- *Remind participants of the tape recording and the need for one person talking at a time.*

- *Request total group involvement. Remind participants that "we want to give everyone a chance to talk."*

- *Delayed response. Some eager respondents want to be the first to answer every question. To avoid this the moderator can simply say, "Let's have someone else go first."*

- *Reseating. The moderator can take a break and tell respondents that everyone is going to take new seats, assigning places. This is particularly helpful in groups where participants hold side conversations.*

- *Flattery. One of the best ways of holding back the "experts" is to recognize their greater familiarity with the subject, asking that they wait until others have answered before responding to questions.*

- *Ejection. This is definitely the technique of last resort. Most commonly, the client or the moderator on a break will ask the host or hostess to come in and call the respondent out of the room.*

## Participant Comments

Several types of comments cause difficulties for the focus group moderator. One category is disrespectful and personal attacks by one participant on another. The second category is incorrect and harmful advice that is offered by one participant to another. A third category includes personal disclosures that are above and beyond what was asked. Let's discuss these one at a time.

### Disrespectful and Personal Attacks

Some topics are emotionally charged. The topic is sensitive, and participants in the group may disagree. At times this can yield a productive and enlightening discussion, but it can also degenerate into disrespectful, personal attacks. The guiding rule in focus groups is that participants listen to each other and be respectful of other views. Often the moderator can anticipate these differences and can discuss them when providing the ground rules: "We anticipate that we might have differing views on this topic. You may hear opinions that you do not agree with, and if this happens, we ask that you respectfully listen and then share your view."

### Incorrect or Harmful Advice

The second area of concern is incorrect or harmful advice that participants share with each other. This occurs more often in studies of technical topics, employee benefits, or subjects like public health. We suggest that the moderator use the following procedure. When something is said that the moderator knows to be incorrect, the moderator considers whether or not the inaccurate information is harmful. Not harmful means that no one is injured directly or indirectly. Such comments may not be comfortable to the moderator because they could be critical of the sponsor, the topic, or the focus group process. Nevertheless, if the comment is not harmful, the moderator takes no action. If, however, the comments could be harmful, the moderator waits until the end of the focus group and brings up the topic again. This time, the moderator presents the topic as a matter of "fact" as opposed to the "opinions" that were shared earlier. The moderator describes the topic, provides the answer, and cites the source. The moderator might even offer to send participants a copy of the information or facts if they are interested. This strategy removes the harmful information from the domain of "opinion," resurfaces it later in the focus group when it has more attention, and provides participants with access to the source data.

EXAMPLE

**Harmful Advice Given in a Focus Group**

*Occasionally participants will share advice in the focus group, and sometimes that advice has the potential for being harmful. Here are some examples we've heard:*

- *"You know, it is really not important to use gloves, mask, and all that stuff when you mix pesticides. My dad has been doing that for years, and it hasn't hurt him a bit."*
- *"When I go camping, I purify my drinking water by adding a small amount of household bleach. Sure, it tastes a little funny, but it really kills the germs."*
- *"At Thanksgiving time my grandmother prepares the turkey at her house and then wraps it up in a roaster with a blanket around it and brings it to our house. She lives about 4 hours away, so we have to reheat it when she arrives."*

### Personal Disclosures

Other problem comments are those that may incriminate the participant or another person. These include accusations of wrongdoing, illegal behavior, or unethical or improper actions. These experiences are best handled by anticipating that they might occur, developing a protocol, and revising questions to minimize the problem. For example, in a study of alcohol use prevention for teens, you might ask about how teens generally obtain alcohol but not ask particular teens if they have personally obtained alcohol. Some topics will evoke stories, and participants may want to share their experiences. In a study of sexual harassment, we might expect that an individual might wish to tell details. If this happens, the story is often regarded as truth and the accused person is considered guilty. In other cases, as in dealing with child abuse, the moderator may be required to report abusive situations to legal authorities. The moderator should be ready for these comments and determine protocol of what to do before they occur. A strategy that we sometimes use is to seek "general" information on topics and to indicate to participants that we do not seek their personal stories. If they wish to share a story and they feel they need to include names, we will encourage them to select from a list of gender-neutral names as they tell their story. We might write several names on the flip chart, such as Pat, Chris, Shawn, or Marty. Then, as the story is told, the participant uses a name from the list to replace the real name.

## Participant Questions

In focus groups, participants sometimes ask questions of the moderator. This should be expected, it is natural, and it can actually be beneficial to the discussion. Questions occur before the focus group, just after the introduction to the focus group, during the focus group, or at the conclusion of the discussion. The strategy of answering differs for each time period. Let's take them one at a time.

*Questions Before the Focus Group.* These questions can occur during the invitation process or just prior to the discussion. They are asked individually, and the strategy of answering should be to provide sufficient information to put the participant at ease. Often the questions are about the purpose of the focus group, who's using the results, or about the timing or location. The principle in responding is to give answers but not to give information that might be leading.

*Questions After the Introduction.* These questions sometimes occur, but don't invite them. The moderator's introduction usually takes only a few minutes, and you should move directly into the round-robin, opening question. The danger in inviting questions at the beginning is that, in responding, the moderator may appear defensive, evasive, and apologetic. It takes only one person to fire off a series of questions that should not or cannot be answered. For example, "Who's going to read the report? What have other groups said? Will decisions be made on what we say? Who's really sponsoring this study? Who really wants this information? Can we see copies of the report? Who's paying for this?" The rule of thumb is not to invite questions, but if someone does ask a question, decide if it should be answered promptly or postponed until later.

*Questions During the Focus Group.* These can relate to a variety of topics or concerns. The moderator will need to consider each of these questions individually. Some should be answered, some should be deflected, and some should be postponed. The four options of answering questions are to turn a question back to the questioner, to invite someone else to answer it, to postpone the answer, or to give an answer.

When questions are asked, think about whether the person is asking a question or making a statement. A number of people make statements by their questions. If you sense that the person really wants to make a point, you might respond with, "Tell me more about that" or "That's a good question, how would you answer it?" or simply "Why do you ask?"

Another strategy is to invite someone else to answer the question. This is often a desirable strategy if the question is about opinions, rather than facts. The important criterion is that the moderator doesn't appear evasive. If the question is specifically directed to the moderator, then it is difficult to give it away.

A third strategy is to postpone the answer. If the topic is going to be discussed in more detail later in the focus group, you might say, "We're going to be talking about that in a few minutes." If the topic is not on the questioning route, you might try, "We'll be talking about things like that at the end. But right now . . ."

The fourth strategy is to answer the question. There may a danger in answering questions relating to opinions, because earlier you've told participants that there are no right or wrong answers. It is desirable to give answers if the question is about a factual matter or is an important foundation to the later discussion.

*Questions at the Conclusion of the Group.* These questions are welcomed and encouraged. If a question was postponed, be sure to bring it up again at the end of the focus group. Questions asked at the end of the focus group can give clues about additional information that you might include in the introduction of future focus groups.

---

**Can I See a Copy of the Final Report?**

*Perhaps the most frequent question asked at focus groups, particularly for public and nonprofit organizations, is "Will we get a copy of the results?" Rarely, if ever, are reports shared in the private market research environment because of the proprietary nature of the results. In fact, considerable care is taken to ensure the secrecy of these results. We've found the opposite to be true in the public sector. Not only is it acceptable to share results, but it is often desirable. Sharing results conveys that you really did listen. It also conveys a sense of openness and fosters positive attitudes that all sides must work together to achieve results. Anticipate this question and discuss it with the sponsoring group. We recommend that you eagerly share copies of the results. To do this, be sure to maintain a listing of names and addresses of all focus group participants.*

---

## Removing Participants From Focus Groups

Occasionally, you'll need to remove someone from a focus group. This could occur at the very beginning when someone shows up, perhaps even invited, but you discover that the person should not be in the group. At other times, you will need to remove someone after the focus group has begun. Let's take these situations one at a time.

*Removing Someone Before the Focus Group Begins.* You may have uninvited guests show up for the focus group. In some situations, we've allowed guests to stay during the focus group session, but it is usually preferable to direct them to a waiting area outside of the room.

For example, suppose an invited senior shows up with a spouse who drove the car. According to the senior, "We do everything together." Depending on circumstances, there might be a chair on the side of the room where the spouse can wait, or perhaps there are chairs outside in a lobby or waiting area. You might offer refreshments and let the guest know where to sit and wait or when to come back. Your response might run like this: "We have a place for you to wait out in the lobby, or if you like, you can come back in two hours. Before you leave, you might wish to have some refreshments."

Sometimes you have an uninvited guest who really wants to listen (and likely participate) in the focus group. Often these people show up for the best of reasons but cause the worst damage. Local reporters may want to cover the focus group for the local media; a chief executive, pastor, or supervisor wants to hear firsthand of the concerns of employees or customers; members of a public interest group or other concerned citizens want to have their views heard on the topic of investigation. They all mean well, but they will interfere with your research in the focus group interview. At times like these, it is critical that the moderator and assistant moderator be sensitive and responsive but also firm and clear. Thank the people for their interest. Praise them for being interested in this important topic. Let them know that this is a research project that requires limited attendance—it is not a public meeting. Only those invited are allowed to participate. If others are present, it will jeopardize the quality of the research. Perhaps, if time permits, you can give a briefing of the study and the early findings after the focus group. Alternatively, you might invite the uninvited guest to share ideas on the topic in writing. Give him or her a blank copy of the question route and your card. Ask the person to fill it out and return it to you in the next week. Offer, if it is reasonable and possible, to send the guest a copy of the final report.

*Removing Someone After the Focus Group Begins.* Still another problem involves removing someone from the focus group after the discussion has begun. This will rarely occur, but when it does, the results can be devastating. Once in a great while, someone will be absolutely intolerant and will not allow others to express their views. He or she will dominate the discussion, and other participants will either get angry or become silent. Sometimes this behavior is the result of excessive alcohol or drugs. Sometimes it just reflects an aggressive, intolerant, and hostile personality.

Sometimes it is the behavior of someone who has spent a lifetime fighting for or against your topic. The strategy that has worked for us is described in the "Tip" box below.

**Removing the Excessively Dominant Individual**

*Once you've realized that a group with this individual cannot be successful, you tell the group, "We've finished with the first part of our discussion, and now we're going to take a short break." During the break, ask the dominating individual to step outside the room or over to the side. Smile, look the person in the eye, be firm, and say, "Our discussion is in two parts and not everyone will be staying for the second part. You are free to leave. We've appreciated hearing your views, and your ideas have been helpful and instructive to us. Thank you for coming." Then offer any incentive that was promised. Shake hands. After a few moments, reconvene the group, but make no mention of the departed participant.*

*You might also consider the more direct approach. This too begins with a break and an opportunity to talk one-to-one with the dominant individual: "We've appreciated that you've shared your views here in our discussion. Your opinions have been helpful to us. However, in the second part of the group it is vital that we hear other points of view. You will not be participating in the second part of our discussion. We thank you for coming."*

*Usually we make no mention of the absent participant when we reconvene the group. If someone asks, we just say, "John will not be participating in the next part of our discussion. He has shared his views, and we've appreciated his input. Now, we want to hear more about your views."*

# 10

# Assistant Moderator Responsibilities

Overview

*Tips on Selecting an Assistant*
*The Role of the Assistant Moderator*

## Tips on Selecting an Assistant

When selecting an assistant moderator, you should consider several factors to maximize the benefit of having an assistant. For example, your assistant can be a detriment if he or she just sits there, takes random notes, and misses important points. The quality of the focus group depends in part on your selection of a competent assistant. Consider the following suggestions.

Select someone with characteristics different from those of the moderator. These differences could be in demographics, language, experiences in the organization, past training, or a host of others. The diversity of the team enhances analysis.

Consider candidates who are concerned about the topic. These individuals are curious and interested. Be careful, however, that they are able to control their reactions to unpopular and negative comments.

Select someone with sufficient self-discipline not to participate in the discussion and yet remain objective and open-minded on the topic. Assistant moderators should be able to control their verbal and nonverbal reactions, no matter how strongly they feel

KEY POINT

**The Diversity of the Team Enhances Analysis**

about an issue. During the focus group, the assistant should expect to talk only if and when invited by the moderator.

## The Role of the Assistant Moderator

By our choice of the title "assistant moderator," we do not wish to imply that the assistant is less important or less vital to the study. The assistant could be referred to as a recorder, observer, analyst, or even consultant, but these titles also have limitations. The assistant has several special functions that are critical to success. The moderator and the assistant moderator are members of a team. With this team approach, each individual has certain tasks to perform. The moderator is concerned primarily with directing the discussion and keeping the conversation flowing and on topic. The notes taken by the moderator are not so much to capture the total interview but rather to identify a few key ideas or future questions that need to be asked. The assistant, on the other hand, takes comprehensive notes, operates the tape recorder, handles environmental conditions and logistics (refreshments, lighting, seating, etc.), and responds to unexpected interruptions. In addition, the assistant notes the participants' body language throughout the discussion. Occasionally, the assistant will ask additional questions near the end of the discussion or probe the response of a participant in more depth. The assistant is also extremely helpful in the post-meeting analysis of the session.

The assistant moderator is not usually used in private sector market research projects unless as an apprentice in training. This limited use of assistant moderators in market research is due to additional labor costs. We have found assistant moderators well worth the investment. A second set of eyes and ears increases both the total accumulation of information and the validity of the analysis. Furthermore, an assistant provides a means for dealing with distracting interruptions to the focus group interview, such as late arrivals, unwanted background music, or the need to switch tapes.

Public and nonprofit organizations have a potential advantage in the use of assistant moderators. Within many organizations there are individuals who, motivated by curiosity or concern, are willing to "sit in" on the focus group and to help with assigned functions. In some circumstances, these individuals may have background characteristics similar to those of the participants. As a result, they may offer valuable assistance in analysis. Some care must be taken to ensure that the newly recruited assistant moderator understands the roles and responsibilities and doesn't inadvertently upstage the focus group. This potential problem can be solved by explicitly outlining the purpose and rules of the session.

**The Role of
the Assistant**

*A moderator was conducting a series of focus group on the quality of groundwater in various places around the United States. We invited local university experts in water quality to serve as assistants, because the action plan that was to follow would require planning and training from these professors. In one state, the professor serving as assistant moderator wasn't able to control his response to the lack of information and the misinformation of the participants. Halfway through the focus group, he stood up and told the participants that they were all wrong in their knowledge of water. He then proceeded to give a mini-lecture on ground water quality. Needless to say, the participants were no longer interested in talking after being scolded and lectured.*

*We learned an important lesson. In future focus groups, the assistants were given clear and explicit instruction as to when they could talk and what they could say. We wanted their wisdom in interpreting the results, not in teaching the participants.*

### Assist With Logistics

- Be responsible for equipment. The assistant should be familiar with the equipment and how it is set up, as well as common problems and solutions in working with equipment, including recorders, microphone, tapes, and flip charts.
- Be responsible for refreshments. Arrange for food (either complete meals or snacks) and beverages. Ensure that refreshments are available on time and in sufficient quantity.
- Arrange the room. Arrange chairs and tables. Be attentive to background noises that can affect the audio recording, as well as to room temperature and lighting.
- Handle paperwork. Coordinate the registration process. Be sure that handouts are available and all reporting forms are collected. Distribute honorariums and collect receipt signatures.

TIP

**Handling
Honorariums**

*Here's how we distribute focus group honorariums. The honorariums are given out at the end of the focus group. Usually these consist of cash, not checks, and are placed in envelopes with the names of the participants written on the outside. The participants are asked to sign that they have received the money. We prepare a tablet listing each person's name. On the top of the page, it says, "I have received $25 for participating in the focus group interview at (location) on (date)." The moderator is expected to account for all funds, either by returning the envelopes or by having the participants' signatures on the receipt list.*

**BACKGROUND**

**The Financial Incentive—What Do You Call It?**

*What do you call the money given to focus group participants? In market research groups, it might be called an honorarium or a co-op fee. We've found that we regularly need a variety of names, depending on the sponsoring organization. Most often, we'll call the money an honorarium, but sometimes it is called a travel expense, average reimbursement for travel, participation fee, per diem, miscellaneous research expense, or some other name. We've had to use different names because of the traditions and accounting procedures of public and nonprofit organizations. These organizations and institutions have precise procedures for paying people (salary, consultation, honorariums, etc.), and, by and large, they are not accustomed to paying people for research costs. Categories just don't exist for paying people to attend focus groups. As a result, internal accountants often ask lots of questions about the study. We've found that we need names that already exist in the accountant's lexicon. Pick your words carefully. Be ready for this, and use careful practices for accounting for the funds.*

**BACKGROUND**

**Why Do We Pay People to Attend Focus Groups?**

*This question gets asked regularly in the public and nonprofit sectors. The question runs, "We don't pay people to participate in other forms of research or to go to meetings, so why should we pay people for attending focus groups?" You need to have an answer! Here are several to consider.*

*First, there is a tradition within focus group research to compensate participants financially. Not paying people clearly goes against this tradition. People know of the inconvenience demanded, expect to be paid, and might not attend unless you pay.*

*Second, paying people to attend actually saves money. Paying people ensures attendance, reduces recruiting costs, and avoids costs associated with rescheduling groups.*

*Third, focus group research is more demanding of participants than other forms of inquiry. When you use a mail-out survey, individuals can complete it in their homes, whenever they want. When you do a telephone interview, the person stays at home or at work. When you conduct an individual interview, you go to a place convenient to the person being interviewed. But in focus groups, the people must travel to a location you designate, when you designate, and for the length of time you designate. It is clearly a greater inconvenience for participants than other forms of inquiry.*

*Fourth, payment is insurance that people will attend and that the research can be conducted. People must attend for you to conduct focus groups. Without people attending, all time and costs incurred are wasted.*

**Monitor the Entrance and Handle Interruptions**

- Serve as host. Welcome participants as they arrive. Make participants feel comfortable and appreciated.
- Serve as doorkeeper. Close the door when the focus group is about to begin. Control access to the focus group room.

- Sit in the designated location. Sit outside the circle, preferably opposite the moderator and closest to the door. Greet those arriving late and find them a place to sit.

## Record Discussion

- Take field notes throughout the discussion. These notes should be *word for word* to the extent possible. If the tape doesn't work, these notes will be all you will have for analysis.
- Operate recording equipment. Be familiar with the tape recorder. Turn over or insert another tape as quietly as possible. Label cassette tapes.

## Observe the Discussion

- Observe the focus group and record your observations in field notes.
- Note body language, such as signs of agreement, frustration, and concern.

## Ask Follow-Up Questions

- Ask questions when invited. At the end of the discussion, the moderator may invite you to ask questions for amplification or clarification.

## Offer Oral Summary

- Give an oral summary. At the conclusion of the focus group, provide a brief oral summary (about 3 minutes). Invite participants to offer additions or corrections to the summary.

## Participate in Debriefing

- Debrief with moderator. Discuss overall impressions, notable quotes, key ideas or insights presented, and how this group compared with other groups.

## Assist With Analysis

- Give feedback on analysis and reports. Be the first reader of all reports. Review reports carefully, and suggest changes or additions as needed.

Note Suggestions for Giving an Oral Summary in Chapter 4 of *Developing Questions for Focus Groups*

# 11

# Taking Notes
# and Recording
# the Discussion

### Overview
*Note Taking*
*Flip Charts*
*Electronic Recording*

Focus group sessions are typically recorded in several ways: by field notes taken by an assistant moderator, by flip charts, and by a tape recorder. Written field notes are essential. Typically, the moderator will take brief notes, and the assistant will attempt to capture complete statements of the participants—especially those comments that may be quotable. The moderator's note taking should not interfere with the spontaneous nature of the group interview, and the moderator will be able to capture only brief comments by the participants. If the group has to wait until the moderator finishes taking notes, the discussion will hardly be comfortable, free-flowing, and relaxed.

The note taking should be done in such a manner that the notes are complete and usable if the tape recorder stops working. Tape recorders shouldn't be completely trusted. Murphy's Law dictates that the most insightful comment will be lost when the tape is being switched or when background noise drowns out voices on the tape. At other times, the moderator and assistant moderator may get so involved in the discussion that they both forget to monitor the tape recorder.

## Note Taking

Note taking is a primary responsibility of the assistant moderator. The moderator should not be expected to take written notes during the discussion. Typically, the field notes taken by a moderator are used just for the purposes of the discussion—to reweave comments, to remember points that should be discussed later, or to capture comments that need further explanation. As a result, the assistant moderator plays a critical role in capturing, on paper, the central points of the discussion.

Here are some points to consider in taking field notes on a focus group:

• Strive for clarity and consistency. Anticipate that others will need to use your field notes. Field notes sometimes are reviewed and interpreted days or weeks after the focus group, and by then memory has faded. Consistency and clarity are essential for identifying quotes, summary points, and observations. Consider using a standardized reporting form, especially as you begin your experience with taking field notes.

**Note the Example of the Standardized Reporting Form Later in This Chapter**

• Field notes contain different types of information. It is essential that these different categories of information be easily identified and organized. For example, your field notes will contain quotes, paraphrased quotes, summary points or themes, questions that occur to the recorder, big ideas that affect the study, observations on body language or discussion climate, etc. Confusion can result unless the researchers can readily separate this information.

Develop a scheme to separate this information. The Standardized Reporting Form might be considered (see the example on pages 79-80), or you could just draw a line down the middle of the page and label the right side "quotes" and the left side "key points." Note the following style suggestions for note-taking procedures.

| Note-Taking Style Suggestions | |
|---|---|
| Quotes | Capture these word for word on right side of page. |
| Paraphrased quotes | Capture key phrases word for word. Use ellipses ( . . . ) to indicate that words are missing. Quotes and paraphrased quotes are the *only* information placed on the right side of page. |
| Summary points or themes | List these on the left side of the page. |
| Major themes | Place a star or check mark by these themes. |
| Questions that occur to the recorder | These questions might be asked later and are identified with a question mark at the beginning and end of the question, for example, ?This is an example of the style? These questions are placed on the left side of the notes. |
| Big ideas that affect the study | These thoughts and interpretations of the assistant moderator are circled and placed on the left side. |
| Observations on body language, discussion climate, etc. | These observations are placed on the left side, and a box is drawn around each observation. |
| Sketch of the seating pattern | Sketch this on the back side of the field notes or at the top or bottom of the first page of field notes. |

**Note-Taking Style**

• Draw a sketch of the seating arrangement. The assistant should sketch out the seating order around the table. In the debriefing following the focus group and in later analysis, the team might forget names but might remember that it was the person across the table, or the second person from the right. As a result, this sketch can serve to jog the memory for later discussion and analysis.

• Capture quotes. Listen for notable quotes, the well-said statements that illustrate important points of view. Listen for sentences or phrases that are particularly enlightening or that eloquently express a particular point of view. Place the name, initial, or code number of the speaker after the quotations. Usually, it's impossible to capture the entire quote, so capture as much as you can with attention to the key phrases. Use an ellipsis ( . . . ) to indicate that part of the quote is missing.

- Highlight key points and themes for each question. Typically, participants will talk about several key points in response to each question. Several different participants may offer the same key points. Often these points are distinguished by the frequency with which they are mentioned, although sometimes they are said only once but in a manner that deserves attention. At the end of the focus group, the assistant moderator will share these themes with participants for confirmation.

- Jot down follow-up questions that could be asked. Sometimes the moderator may not follow up on an important point or seek an example of a vague but critical point. The assistant moderator may wish to follow-up with these questions at the end of the focus group.

- Write down your big ideas, hunches, or thoughts. Occasionally the assistant moderator will discover a new concept. A light will go on, and something will make sense when before it did not. These insights are helpful in later analysis.

- Note other factors that might aid analysis, such as passionate comments, body language, or nonverbal activity. Watch for head nods, physical excitement, eye contact between certain participants, or other clues that would indicate the level of agreement, support, or interest. (See the "Caution" on body language on page 79.)

- Always remember the purpose of the focus group. It is easy to get sidetracked on interesting but irrelevant topics. Throughout the conversation, the assistant must continually compare what is being said with the purpose of the study. This means that some questions are more important than others. As a result, limited or no notes are needed on some topics, while copious notes are needed on others.

A strategy that will help with note taking is to attempt to capture a transcript while the group is talking. In the past several years, laptop computers have offered portability and silence. A fast typist is sometimes able to capture a nearly complete transcript of the focus group while the group is being conducted.

If you decide to use this strategy, be sure the typist is slightly away from the table, so as not to disturb the participants with keyboard sounds, yet close enough to hear everything that is being said.

*Keep body language in perspective. Consider it, but don't overinterpret it. Experts who study body language often have had the opportunity to observe an individual over a considerable period of time and in differing circumstances. In a focus group you may never have seen this person before, and, therefore, you'll have no baseline for comparison. Instead, watch for obvious signals such as head nods of agreement, eye contact, or hand movement indicating a desire to talk, physical withdrawal from the group, and so forth. If the body language is important, ask participants to comment. For example, "I saw that several of you nodded your heads when Jane talked about morale factors. Would any of you like to comment?" For more discussion about body language and nonverbal communication, see Volume 6 in this series,* Analyzing and Reporting Focus Group Results.

**Don't Get Too Serious About Body Language**

*Here's an example of a reporting form for field notes. We construct these using our word processor and find them very helpful for beginning assistant moderators.*

EXAMPLE

**Standardized Reporting Form**

## Information About the Focus Group

| | |
|---|---|
| Date of Focus Group | |
| Location of Focus Group | |
| Number and Description of Participants | |
| Moderator Name | |
| Assistant Moderator Name | |

## Responses to Questions

Q1. When you hear the term *customer service*, what comes to mind?

| Brief Summary/Key Points | Notable Quotes |
|---|---|
| | |
| Comments/Observations | |
| | |

Q2. Describe exceptionally good service.

| Brief Summary/Key Points | Notable Quotes |
|---|---|
| | |
| Comments/Observations | |
| | |

Q3. Describe exceptionally poor service.

| Brief Summary/Key Points | Notable Quotes |
|---|---|
| | |
| Comments/Observations | |
| | |

## Flip Charts

Another way to capture information is through the use of flip charts. Thought should be given to how their use affects participants. At their worst, flip charts can slow down the conversation, and, in the process, participants forget their ideas because they are waiting for the writer to capture the thought. Because the participant's comment must be written quickly, it must be truncated and critical elements may be lost. At their best, flip charts help participants stay on topic and remember what others have said. The guiding rule I follow is to use the flip chart for lists that must be remembered and when it is important to acknowledge visibly to participants that you have captured their comments.

Sometimes people talk in phrases rather than sentences when flip charts are used. The moderator must encourage participants to continue talking while he or she is writing and must elicit sufficient examples and descriptions of items listed. Sometimes the comments are superficial and need further probing to be helpful. For example, in a recent study we asked hospital patients to list what they wanted in a caregiver. The patients said they wanted someone "to care" or "to listen," plus a number of other, rather cryptic comments. After a few moments, the flip chart was filled with comments. The moderator then went through the items on the flip chart, one at a time, and asked how people could tell when someone really was doing these things. What were the behaviors of the caregiver? In this case, the flip chart was a valuable means of listing qualities, which could then be discussed in greater depth.

## Electronic Recording

Tape recorders are invaluable and a must for focus group interviews. The tape recording equipment and remote microphone are set up in plain sight before the meeting begins. Hidden recorders and microphones are usually unwise, because they create an unnecessarily secretive atmosphere and inhibit participant conversation if discovered. Therefore, it is best to have the recording equipment in full view of the participants. The importance of the recorder is mentioned at the beginning of the group discussion, and it is introduced as a tool to help capture everyone's comments. Participants are encouraged to speak one at a time to avoid garbling the tape.

---

*Certain noises in the focus group make tape recording exceedingly difficult. You may not even notice these sounds until you listen to the tape recording and discover that portions of the tape are unintelligible. Here are some culprits to listen for:*

**Noise Distractions**

- *Drumming of fingers near the microphone*
- *Tapping of pencils or pens on the table*
- *Tapping of feet on table legs*
- *Hum of heating or air conditioning systems*
- *Background music*

*By watching for these potential noise distractions, the moderator can sometimes take steps to ensure quality recording. Such action may be as simple as asking, "You know, we want to be able to tape record all comments, and because our microphone is particularly sensitive, tapping on the table makes it impossible to hear what people are saying. So, please don't tap on the table."*

---

Care is needed to avoid drawing excessive attention to the tape recording. Occasionally a novice moderator will comment at length about the tape recording: that the comments are confidential, that no names will be used in the report, that there is no need to worry, and so on. The moderator inadvertently creates an environment that restricts the free flow of information by giving too much attention to the recording. It is best to mention that recording is taking place and that no names will be included in reports, and then move on to the next topic. In some situations, the tape recording is perceived as symbolic of careful listening.

---

EXAMPLE

**The Influence of the Microphone**

*Recently, a large school system conducted focus groups on merit pay for teachers—a sensitive topic to many teachers. In the planning phase, concern was expressed about the wisdom of tape recording and about whether it would inhibit conversation. The decision was made to try it out and then, if necessary, turn off the recording equipment. When the teachers arrived in the room, someone promptly commented that "finally the school administration is taking the opinions of teachers seriously." The moderator asked the teacher to comment further. The teacher replied, "Well, you're tape recording our comments! All along the school administrators said they were listening, and we knew they weren't because they didn't record, take notes, or anything. Now it looks like they're serious about listening." Indeed, throughout that and future focus groups, the teachers would lean toward the microphone in the center of the table when topics of concern were addressed and would talk more slowly so that their comments would be clearly understood.*

---

Tape recording group conversations is difficult because recorders are prone to pick up background noise, tapping of pencils, and the hum of the ventilation system instead of the softly spoken comments of participants. Built-in microphones on cassette recorders tend to have limited sensitivity. For better results, an omnidirectional remote microphone should be placed in the center of the table. Recently some moderators have had considerable success with pressure-sensitive microphones that pick up sound vibrations from the table. These microphones are called "PZM" for pressure zone microphone. Occasionally, moderators use two microphones placed at different ends of the table and each connected to a recorder. Immediately before the group interview, the moderator should again test the recording equipment to be sure that all comments in the room will be captured, even if spoken in quiet tones. In addition, the moderator may want to fast forward and rewind new tapes to ensure that they do not stick or jam. The C-90 tapes are preferable; C-60 tapes are too short, and C-120 tapes are more prone to break and jam.

The C-90 tape provides 90 minutes of recording time, 45 minutes per side. We have had problems reusing tapes, so we always use new tapes for focus groups. The $2.00 spent on a new tape is insignificant compared with the cost of conducting the group.

*Here's an easy way to identify quality tapes. Just look at the price. Price is generally a good indicator of quality in cassette tapes. The highest priced tapes are often used for recording music, but the extra cost may not add to the quality of the voice sounds. Avoid low-cost tapes because they are more prone to breakage.*

**TIP**

**Use Quality Tapes**

We have avoided videotaping groups, but for a different reason. Videotaping is obtrusive and usually not worth the effort. We have found that the video camera may change the environment and affect participant spontaneity. Videotaping usually requires several cameras plus camera operators who attempt to swing cameras quickly to follow the flowing conversation. The fuss and fury of videotaping makes the focus group appear more like a circus than a discussion.

*Carol Bryant from the University of South Florida tells about an innovative strategy for using videotapes of focus groups. Several years ago, she conducted a study on breast-feeding that included over a dozen focus groups with women participating in the Special Supplemental Nutrition Program for Women, Infants and Children (WIC). Research pointed to the importance of peers as information sources about breast-feeding and about ways of overcoming obstacles, such as embarrassment about nursing in public. The researchers decided to capture the richness of the information the women shared in the focus group discussions on video, but they did not want the equipment to interfere with the discussion. They decided to add several additional groups at the end of the study so that they could videotape them. WIC participants were asked to attend a group discussion in a small film studio and were told that they would be filmed. Everything else remained consistent with earlier groups. As expected, the comments resembled those in earlier groups. After about 10 minutes, the women seemed to ignore the cameras and discussed the issues in the same way as women had in previous groups. Because the group content was similar, researchers were able to select comments representing major research themes (breast-feeding barriers and advice about how to overcome them). These video clips were then edited into a promotional videotape for distribution to WIC programs around the country. The videotape has proven successful, in large part because viewers can identify with the focus group speakers (also WIC participants) and the concerns that they discuss on the tape. Because of the tapes' success, focus group research and subsequent videotaping have been used to develop four additional breast-feeding promotion tapes targeting other audience segments.*

**EXAMPLE**

**An Innovative Way to Videotape a Focus Group**

# 12

# The Rapid Focus Group

**Overview**

*Suggestions for Implementing Rapid Focus Groups*
*Questions for Rapid Focus Groups*
*Special Concerns*
*Success Comes From Consistency, Anticipation*
*and Experience*
*Ensuring Moderator Consistency*
*Preparing the Research Team*
*Note Taking in Rapid Focus Groups*

Sooner or later, you'll need to do a rapid focus group. A crisis will emerge, you will need information quickly, and you will rapidly assemble several groups to discuss the problem and solution. The rapid focus group is a focus group specifically adapted to accommodate emerging or immediate situations or opportunities. These quickly assembled focus groups typically have a limited number of questions and require speedy analysis. This section offers some suggestions to help you when you are considering this special type of focus group.

Rapid focus groups tend to be used in situations such as those that follow:

- A formative evaluation is needed for a conference. Rapid focus groups can be held at the end of each day of a multiday conference. Results are compared across groups, and each day conference organizers consider modifications for the coming day.
- An emerging, important topic is added to an existing meeting. A meeting or conference has already been planned, but shortly before the session, a new topic surfaces. The topic is one of concern to decision makers, and they wish to take advantage of the meeting to gain feedback on how to understand the issue or how to respond to the situation.
- A community or organization has an emergency and wants information quickly. Something unusual, unexpected, or drastic has just occurred. The emergency, disaster, or incident requires a rapid response. Decision makers need information about how to handle the matter. Before they take action, they decide to listen and seek options.

The primary advantage of the rapid focus group is its ability to respond quickly from a target audience. Within hours, decision makers have results, and action can begin. Another advantage is the timing. In certain situations, there is a narrow window of opportunity in which to act on a particular problem, and delay may be either impossible or undesirable. The time may be ideal for discussion because people often are motivated, concerned, or at least interested in the topic. Enthusiasm may run high, and there is often a tendency for participants to encourage immediate action.

The rapid focus group is *not* a normal focus group. It is a special adaptation that has clear limits and disadvantages. The topic may become overly simplified, the discussion may be limited, the moderator may not be prepared to follow up on critical topics, and the analysis may have limited depth. Overall, when you use a rapid focus group, you increase your risk of error.

## Suggestions for Implementing Rapid Focus Groups

Here are suggestions to consider when you need to conduct these special groups. These steps may need to occur simultaneously and do not have to be used in the sequence presented here.

### Have a Plan on File

Develop your plan now, before the emergency occurs! When a crisis occurs, there will be general confusion, and it will be difficult to think through a strategy. Develop one or more plans in writing, and make them available to key people. The plan doesn't need to be documented in great detail, but it should provide sufficient information for those around you regarding your intentions, the resources needed, and how others can help. You might begin by thinking about a recent crisis situation and developing a plan for that event. In some organizations, crises occur regularly and seem to follow predictable patterns. Sketch out a plan of action for one of these past events, along with a timetable and budget. Invite others to review the plan, and keep it on file for an upcoming emergency.

### Consider Your Resources

Your major limitation will be resources. These include time, talent, and money. Quickly inventory your resources. How much time do you have? What talents or skills can you draw on? (This is not the best situation in which to conduct your first focus group!) What financial costs (meals, room costs, transportation, incentives, moderator fees, etc.) exist?

### Determine the Number of Rapid Focus Groups Needed

This number will depend on available moderators, the nature of the topic, and the diversity of the participants. How many moderators can you recruit? Seek out people who've had successful experiences with moderating. If experienced moderators are not available, consider recruiting new moderators and invite them to attend a short training session.

Don't be surprised if you are asked to plan for a sizable number of focus groups. Although lots of focus groups are not needed from a research perspective, over-sampling may be beneficial for morale or to provide a widespread sense of ownership and responsibility for the solution. Sometimes organizations will decide that everyone should be included in discussions, because many people need to participate in the healing, resolution, and solution stages.

Information on Teaching Focus Group Skills Is Found in Volume 5, *Involving Community Members in Focus Groups*

### Target Your Participants

Consider how individuals in your target group are similar or different. Do you want to segment participants by age, gender, ethnicity, experience, position, interest, and so on? Should the topic be discussed by mixed groups or by groups with similar backgrounds? The guiding rule of focus groups is homogeneity, but you'll need to consider the basis of that homogeneity. In one study, it might be the experience level of participants, in another gender, in a third geographic background, and in a fourth membership in a community or employment in an organization. Simply put, which people do you want to hear from?

### Determine the Limits on Facilities and Time

Often these rapid groups will piggyback on existing meetings or conferences, and, consequently, you will be limited to certain facilities and meeting times. Because agendas have already been established, you'll be grabbing time where you can—before meetings, over breakfast, at lunch, or at the end of the sessions. In a few situations, the topic may be so important that the planned agenda is suspended in favor of rapid focus groups. Sometimes, your target audience will be available only at a certain time. The time requirement for these rapid focus groups can vary from 45 minutes to 2 hours, with most about an hour in length. It's difficult to predict the time needed, because each topic is unique. Sometimes, it will take longer than expected, as when participants want to share their personal experiences or when they request more background information. At other times, participants quickly move through the questions and conclude within an hour. Room availability and space requirements can affect the number of groups and the size of each group. It is often easier to find discussion space or tables for small groups of three to five participants than it is for normal groups of six to eight participants. Even greater difficulty occurs in finding locations for groups of nine and ten participants.

### Limit the Scope of Your Inquiry

Because you are often grabbing time where you can, you may have limited opportunity for the discussion; thus, your topics must be specific. Time will not permit exploring in-depth alternatives or complex answers. This rapid focus group is really a superficial "first take" that might be examined later in more depth.

### Limit Your Questions

You need to plan fewer questions than in a standard focus group, and these need to be easy to analyze. The questioning route should probably consist of only four to seven questions.

Move into the topic quickly, ask questions that work well in situations with limited amounts of time and favor quick analysis, and include some questions that all participants are expected to answer. To make analysis easier, consider using questions for which answers can be captured on flip charts or response forms. Moderators or notetakers can use flip charts to capture key points of the discussion.

## Consider How to Capture the Information

You may find yourself in a situation where sound conditions simply don't permit recording, such as a large auditorium with many tables of participants talking at the same time or a noisy community center. Nevertheless, seriously consider tape recording the conversations. Think of the tape recordings as insurance. Occasionally, you will find a group so eloquent that you absolutely must transcribe the conversation. This is impossible without a tape recording.

Strive for consistency in note taking. Invite someone to take notes in the focus group, but encourage him or her to use a note-taking style that you can use in analysis. Look over the section on note taking and revise it as needed.

Another possibility is to consider a laptop computer as a means of capturing as much of the conversation as possible. If you have someone who can quickly and proficiently key in data, you might be able to have a nearly complete transcript in real time.

See the Tips on Note Taking in Chapter 11

## Debrief the Team

If you use multiple moderators and conduct simultaneous focus groups, you'll need to consider a debriefing strategy. Assemble the team in a quiet space to reflect on what was said as soon as possible after the groups are completed. Debriefing can occur in several ways, but the most common procedure is to take one question at a time and ask for a summary of responses to that question from each moderator or assistant. Continue until all questions have been summarized. Each person is encouraged to think about similarities and differences as the comments are shared.

## Rapid Analysis and Reporting

The researcher will likely need to report back to the client in a matter of hours instead of days or weeks. This means that the report will consist of highlights, summary points, and possibly a few selected quotes. Save time for this analysis task and begin immediately after the debriefing. Delays in analysis will increase the difficulty of the task.

## Questions for Rapid Focus Groups

The questions in a rapid focus group require special attention. Because of the limited amount of time available, only about half of the questions of a standard focus group are used. These four to seven questions quickly focus on the topic and lend themselves to rapid analysis. As a result, the questions need to be rather specific and can involve the use of rating sheets, flip charts, idea lists, and other strategies that make it easy to capture results.

Consider the possibility of sharing the questions in writing with the focus group participants. This could be done on a page of paper or on a flip chart. Normally this is not done in a focus group because of the potential for limiting responses and having participants skip some topics in favor of subjects of greater interest. In rapid focus groups, however, the questions are fewer, the sequence is logical and apparent, and the list conveys a sense of direction and alerts participants to the time constraints.

Let's examine some sample questions:

---

EXAMPLE

**Rapid Focus
Group Questions**

*EXAMPLE 1*

*Here's the current situation (described briefly).*

1. *What should we be concerned about?*
2. *What additional information is needed?*
3. *Whom should we listen to?*
4. *What options are available to us?*
5. *How should the decision be made?*
6. *If you were making the decision and knew what you know now, what would you decide? (round-robin)*
7. *Any advice to those who have to make the decision?*

*EXAMPLE 2*

*Here's the current situation (described briefly).*

1. *What is the problem?*
2. *Who is affected?*
3. *What might be done?*
4. *What barriers exist?*
5. *What are the incentives?*
6. *Any advice?*

*EXAMPLE 3*

*Here's the current situation (described briefly).*

1. *What's happening with . . .?*
2. *How serious is it, and how much attention should it receive?*
3. *What caused it to happen?*
4. *What's needed now to deal with it?*
5. *What can each of us do?*
6. *What can we do together as a group or community?*

*EXAMPLE 4*

*Here's the current situation (described briefly).*

1. *How would you describe the current situation?*
2. *Here are several solution strategies. Look them over.*
3. *What are advantages of each?*
4. *What are disadvantages of each?*
5. *If you had to pick one, which would it be?*
6. *What will it take for this to work?*

---

## Special Concerns

Before you undertake a series of rapid focus groups, consider what might go wrong. By anticipating and thinking about these possibilities, you will be better able to deal with a situation when it arises. Think about the following:

- What is the potential that rapid focus groups might fuel a controversy or make a problem worse?
- What if the topic becomes so compelling that it upstages everything else at the meeting or conference?
- What if participants do not show respect for the values and opinions of others?
- What if a moderator encounters hostility, bullying, condescension, aloofness, or other behaviors that limit communication?
- What if the moderator encounters indifference and apathy?
- What if the moderator gets asked lots of questions?

## Success Comes From Consistency, Anticipation, and Experience

Rapid focus groups work better when three factors are present. First, consistency is essential. The moderators' introductions must describe the task in similar ways, the questions must be consistent across focus groups, and the moderators must use similar strategies of moderating and capturing information. Your task is to compare and contrast results across groups, and this is impossible without consistency in your process. Consistency occurs by establishing standard operating procedures and by training the team. These tasks will be discussed below.

The second factor is anticipation. Rapid groups are often considered when pressure is already intense. An emergency has occurred, people are stressed, and sound and careful thinking gives way to rapid action. It's difficult in the heat of the moment to develop a plan that is carefully thought through. Therefore, anticipate and plan in advance. Note the earlier suggestion to "have a plan on file."

The third factor is experience. Develop and nurture a team of colleagues, volunteers, or freelance employees who can be available on short notice. For example, if you regularly do focus groups, invite new people to watch you and help out as assistant moderators. Serve as a mentor to others in your organization or community. Then, when a problem emerges, you'll have a crew of moderators from which to select.

## Ensuring Moderator Consistency

When working with a team of moderators, it is vital to have consistency. Look over the following "standard operating procedures" and adapt these to fit your situation. Then look over the suggestions on preparing and training the team of moderators.

---

EXAMPLE

**Standard Operating Procedures for Moderators in Rapid Focus Groups**

1. *Be comfortable with the questions. Read through the questions several times to be sure you know exactly what is being asked. Practice asking the questions to someone else before you conduct the focus group. Practice with another member of the research team, your spouse, a friend, etc. Avoid reading questions word for word in the focus group. Glance at the question and then look directly at someone and ask the question as best you can. Before you begin the group, think about the possible answer you might get for each question.*

2. *Know the time limits. Be clear about the starting time and the concluding time. How many people are needed, or how long will you wait for more participants before you begin the discussion? Since these are short groups, don't wait too long. Usually the ending time for your rapid focus group is absolute because another activity or event is planned.*

3. *Know how to introduce the topic. Practice the introduction several times. If possible, the team leader should prepare a written introduction to the focus group. Read it several times, and be completely comfortable with the words. Make your own bulleted points and practice using the bullets. Maintain eye contact as you present the points.*

4. *Hold back your personal opinions. You are not there to share how you personally feel about the topic. You are there to listen.*

5. *Be careful about correcting "wrong comments." Sometimes you will hear something that, to you, is clearly incorrect. Do not make corrections, because too often what is either incorrect or correct is merely an opinion or value judgment. The exception is to make corrections when someone says something that is potentially harmful. When this occurs, wait until the end of the group and make the correction. For more information about handling harmful comments, review Chapter 9 of this book.*

6. *Avoid showing approval or disapproval. Be cautious of intentional or accidental responses that indicate approval or disapproval. Such responses can be subtle, like selective smiles or nods, or overt, such as verbal comments ("great," "excellent," etc.).*

7. *Give everyone an opportunity to respond. If someone doesn't talk, explicitly invite that individual to comment. Get the group involved in the discussion.*

8. *Listen for answers. Did the group answer the question? If not, repeat or rephrase the question. Don't assume that talking is the same as answering the question. You want answers to your question, not merely chatter.*

9. *Probe. If someone makes a vague or ambiguous comment, ask for an example or an explanation. Don't probe all comments but, rather, those central to the purpose.*

10. *Debrief. Participate in the debriefing with the entire research team as soon as possible after the groups have concluded. Listen to the results from other groups, and compare and contrast these findings with those from your group.*

---

## Preparing the Research Team

Your guiding objective in preparing the research team is to ensure the consistency of the entire process, given a limited amount of time and with team members who may be unfamiliar to each other. The following process steps may help you in preparing and training the team:

1. Review the standard operating procedures listed above and adapt them to your study.
2. Identify expectations and responsibilities of the research team. It is essential that you clarify the responsibilities of the moderator and the notetaker before you begin recruiting.

3. Recruit moderators and, if needed, notetakers at the rapid focus groups.
4. Train the team members. If they haven't had previous experience with focus groups, you'll need to offer a crash course on the basics of moderating. If they are veteran moderators, then your orientation will include steps 5 through 9 below.
5. Review the purpose of the study and the logistics of the rapid focus groups.
6. Share a recommended standard introduction that the team might use in starting each focus group.
7. Look over the questions. Moderators should practice asking questions of each other. Think about the range of responses. Be ready to probe beyond respondents' superficial answers. In general, moderators should be comfortable with the questions.
8. Review the procedures for capturing information.
9. Describe the analysis strategy (immediate debriefing using notes and flip charts, followed by preparation of a short summary report).

## Note Taking in Rapid Focus Groups

Review the Tips on Note Taking Included in Chapter 11 of This volume

Part of preparing the research team is to ensure that participants' comments are captured in a form that will be useful for rapid analysis. A critical step is to strive for consistency in style. Nothing is more frustrating than needing to make sense out of a study in which a dozen notetakers have all used a different note-taking style. Here are some guidelines to offer those planning to take notes.

Tips on Note Taking

- *Assume that someone else will be using your notes. Use the note-taking style recommended by your team leader.*
- *Capture notable quotes. These are the well-said statements that illustrate important points of view.*
- *Identify key points and themes for each question.*
- *Write down your big ideas, hunches, or thoughts.*
- *Note climate factors—body language, emotions, mood, etc.*
- *Remember the purpose—don't get sidetracked on interesting but irrelevant topics.*
- *Strive for clarity and consistency.*

# 13

# Rate Yourself
## Check Sheets for Moderating

W e frequently hear questions like "How am I doing?" or "What do I need to do to improve?" We offer several rating systems for your consideration. Each reflects considerable experience on the part of the developers. Look over the criteria on each system and select those that best meet your needs. You'll notice that there is a fair amount of redundancy in the different systems. Pay particular attention to areas of commonality, for they represent criteria that cut across the different types of focus group interviews.

As you proceed, here are several points to remember.

- Not all items are of equivalent importance. We have struggled with this issue, and we've decided that, because focus group interviews are sufficiently diverse in purpose, design, and composition, consistent weighting of criteria could be misleading. The weight of one item over another will change from one group to another. For example, in one group the presence of clear rules might be of considerable importance, but in the second study the rules might be of minor importance.

• Many criteria are judgments or perceptions, or are poorly structured and therefore able to be met in differing ways. What is meant by maintaining control in one group might be different in another. Whether the moderator is relaxed and friendly is a matter of perception.

• You may not be in the best position to judge yourself. Consider inviting others to rate you. Your rating could be done by a colleague, a mentor, the sponsor, or even the focus group participants.

The following rating systems may be helpful to you for diagnostic purposes or as a reminder of recommended moderator behavior. It's a mistake to take them too literally, however, or to assume they contain absolute truth. Be flexible and learn what you can from them.

---

**CHECKLIST**

---

**Moderator Rating Sheet From Richard Krueger**

Before the focus group:

☐ *Is familiar with topic and goals of the sponsor.*
☐ *Understands the purpose and objective of each question.*
☐ *Has a sense of the amount of time needed for each question.*
☐ *Anticipates topics of discussion and potential areas of probing.*
☐ *Is mentally and physically ready to act as moderator.*
☐ *Has sufficient technical knowledge of topic.*

During the focus group:

☐ *Delivers a smooth, comfortable introduction that is accurate and complete, including*
  • *a welcome,*
  • *a brief overview of the topic that defines the purpose for the group,*
  • *a description of the ground rules, and*
  • *the opening question.*
☐ *Establishes rapport with participants.*
☐ *Keeps discussion on track and keeps participants involved.*
☐ *Listens carefully; synthesizes information and feeds it back; probes for clarification; gets people to talk.*
☐ *Seeks out both cognitive and affective domains; gets participants to tell both how they think and how they feel about the topic.*
☐ *Handles different participants adeptly; conveys sense of relaxed informality.*
☐ *Brings closure to the group with summary and invites comments on any missing points.*
☐ *Goes to the door and thanks each person individually for coming, just as you would when guests leave your home.*

After the focus group:

- ☐ *Debriefs soon after the focus group with assistant moderator.*
- ☐ *Performs the analysis or provides insight into the analysis.*
- ☐ *Reviews the report for accuracy.*

---

What should an observer look for in a moderator?

1. *Give clear ground rules/purpose statement/full disclosure about mirrors/ microphones/observers/stipends?*
2. *Establish and maintain rapport, and create a "safe place" for respondents to share POBAs (Perceptions, Opinions, Beliefs and Attitudes)?*
3. *Flow from point to point without abrupt shifts?*
4. *Keep the discussion "on purpose" and moving along?*
5. *Probe for clarity?*
6. *Maintain UPR (Unconditional Positive Regard)?*
7. *Ask questions that open up respondents so they can give full answers?*
8. *Avoid leading the respondents (i.e. putting words in their mouths or inappropriate summarize/paraphrase)?*
9. *Include everyone in the discussion?*
10. *Avoid "serial interviewing"?*
11. *Read the room, stay with the respondents, keep attention off of self and the guide?*
12. *Keep self/ego out of the discussion and avoid talking too much?*
13. *Attend to nonverbal communications?*
14. *Use a variety of techniques to promote discussion?*
15. *Pace/lead respondents?*
16. *Listen rather than inform participants?*
17. *Vary voice tone during process?*
18. *Change locations/body positions during discussion?*
19. *Give clear instructions/directions to respondents?*
20. *Provide linking and logic tracking for respondents and observers?*

—Henderson (1991, p. 39)

CHECKLIST

**Checklist for Moderators From Naomi Henderson**

---

Moderator Evaluation

*A. Moderator's preparation*

- *Understands the background and subject matter of the project*
- *Understands the research objectives*
- *Has collected all the sponsor's ideas*
- *Helped develop the topic guide*
- *Has the topic guide memorized*
- *Was ready before the group assembled*

CHECKLIST

**Checklist for Moderators From Mary Debus**

*B. Moderator's manner*

- *Is relaxed and friendly*
- *Stimulates group interaction*
- *Generates enthusiasm and involvement*
- *Listens constructively*
- *Displays warmth and empathy*
- *Is nonjudgmental*
- *Probes without leading*
- *Conveys "incomplete understanding" effectively*
- *Is sensitive to the level of group disclosure*
- *Blends in, but controls*
- *Improvises when necessary*
- *Is flexible when pursuing new ideas*
- *Discusses, but does not question*
- *Displays neutral body language and facial expressions*

*C. Moderator's handling of group influences*

- *Discourages simultaneous talking*
- *Retains group spontaneity*
- *Discourages irrelevant conversation*
- *Discourages intellectualizing by respondents*
- *Permits individual differences of opinion*
- *Brings shy or unresponsive group members into the discussion*
- *Controls dominant or disruptive group members*

Structure of the Group Discussion

*Introduction: Moderator's opening*

- *Put the respondents at ease*
- *Explained the general purpose of the group*
- *Encouraged conflicting opinions*
- *Established moderator neutrality*
- *Established openness: no right or wrong answers*
- *Gave group "rules"*
- *Began developing a rapport with the respondents*
- *Provided a smooth transition to the next phase*

*Phase I: Warm-up*

- *Established a good rapport with the respondents*
- *Obtained necessary background information*

- Began stimulating group interaction
- Gave all respondents an opportunity to speak
- Successfully diminished speech anxiety
- Established the group as a "safe place"
- Enabled group members to know each other
- Stayed within the time limits
- Provided a smooth transition to the next phase

*Phase II: Body of the group discussion*

- Moved from the general to the specific
- Did not disclose key issues prematurely
- Obtained a depth of response to key issues
- Obtained members' true feelings about topics
- Linked information into a cohesive whole
- Exhibited appropriate facilitating behavior
- Exhibited appropriate controlling behavior
- Provided a smooth transition to the next phase

*Phase III: Closure*

- Identified key themes
- Summarized key ideas
- Revealed the strength of attitudes
- Consolidated group feelings about issues
- Identified individual differences of opinion
- Gathered all respondent comments

—Debus (1986, pp. 44-45)

---

These questions are relevant both for evaluating your existing moderator and for determining whether a new person is appropriate.

- What is the moderator's level of experience?
- Does the moderator help plan the research project, or simply execute the research the client specifies?
- Does the moderator prepare a detailed guide well in advance of the groups?
- Does the moderator adequately prepare for the sessions?
- Does the moderator offer "added value" beyond moderating the session?
- Is the moderator up-to-date on new techniques in focus group moderating?
- Does the moderator adequately cover all the material in the guide?
- Does the moderator maintain an appropriate balance between leading the discussion and letting it run out of control?

CHECKLIST

**Evaluating Moderators From Thomas Greenbaum**

- *Does the moderator take responsibility for managing the entire research process?*
- *Does the moderator have an adequate sense of urgency about completing the report?*
- *Does the moderator have the energy and enthusiasm to keep participants interested, even when the hour is late?*

—Greenbaum (1993, pp. 82-85)

# 14

# Improving Your Moderating Skills

## Overview

Suppose that you want to improve your moderating skills. What might you do? Your skill in doing focus groups may not improve by practice alone. Indeed, practice doesn't make perfect if you are practicing the wrong skills. Practice just makes for deeper ruts. Here are some strategies that may guide you as they have helped us develop our skills.

## Get Feedback From a Coach or Mentor

Pick your coach carefully. Locate someone who is skillful with focus groups and with whom you are comfortable. Watch her or him moderate a focus group and then trade places. Ask for feedback. Give thought to how you locate and convince the coach or mentor to help you. What do you have to offer a prospective coach? Why should he or she spend time with you? Being a coach is time-consuming. The coach doesn't know you, may not feel comfortable with teaching, and may find that coaching reduces his or her profitability because he or she is helping you instead of attending to regular business. The frustration of being a coach is that the aggressive people who seek out help may not have the talents for conducting focus groups. Therefore, coaches tend to get more requests from people with limited skills. Those qualities that make certain people brilliant at moderating may be the very reasons that they are reluctant to seek a coach.

Do your homework on the coach. Why is he or she so good? How do you know it? Does the potential coach know people who can open doors for you? First impressions are important because you may not get a second chance. Read about focus groups and study the area of specialization of prospective coaches. Think how you can lighten their load. Can you offer to assist with a difficult task? Can you take notes, serve snacks, prepare analysis, or do something that makes you a asset, not a liability?

## Type Your Own Transcripts

Listen to yourself moderate and type your own comments word for word. Type absolutely everything you say and agonize over it. Was it needed? Should you have said more, followed up on a topic, moved more quickly or more slowly? Did you lead the participants into making certain comments or unduly influence their reactions in other ways? These observations are often missed when someone else types the transcript. When you do it yourself, it gets personal.

## Listen to Yourself and Follow the Transcript

This exercise is similar to the exercise above and can be used if the transcript was prepared by someone else. In this exercise, the moderator listens to himself or herself on tape and follows along in the transcript. Once again, you get a sense of the needless comments you made, the irrelevant discussion you encouraged, and the opportunities you missed.

## Videotape Yourself Moderating

Videotape yourself moderating a focus group. Place the video camera at eye level and tell the participants that because you are interested in improving your skills, the camera is pointed just at you. At the end of the focus group, ask participants for advice. Later, watch the videotape and critique yourself. Invite your mentor or coach to help you critique yourself.

## Observe Others Conducting Focus Groups

Watch a variety of other moderators conduct focus groups. Occasionally, you'll be able to watch (and participate) in a focus group led by a veteran moderator. At other times, you'll be an assistant for someone else. Just by having a range of experiences, you'll be able to discover strategies that others use that might also work for you.

## Form a Study or Support Group

Invite a group of colleagues to join you in forming a study group or support group on focus group interviewing. Share readings and experiences; practice conducting focus groups with each other. Videotape your focus groups and offer feedback to each other. Invite outside speakers to join you and offer advice.

## Read About Focus Group Interviewing

Read everything you can about focus group interviewing. Begin with books and move into journals and monographs. Use the Internet to seek out additional references. Check with your local library about doing electronic searches.

## Join a Professional Society or Group

Professional focus group moderators typically belong to one or more professional organizations. Among the most popular is the Qualitative Research Consultants Association (QRCA), which is composed of many private focus group consultants from all over the world. Other organizations include the American Marketing

Association, the American Association for Public Opinion Research, the American Evaluation Association, the American Education Research Association, and professional groups in sociology, business, communications, and related fields.

## Attend Classes on Moderating

Attend classes on focus group moderating. Increasingly, these classes are being offered in colleges and universities as both credit and noncredit opportunities. In addition, several private research firms also sponsor classes on focus group interviewing.

# 15

# Teaching Others to Moderate

### Overview
*Questions and Answers on Teaching Others*

## Questions and Answers on Teaching Others

This chapter is a short preview of another book in the kit, titled *Involving Community Members in Focus Groups*. We've prepared this in a question-and-answer format so you can quickly gain a sense of the main points. If the concept appeals to you, get the details from the book on teaching others.

Q: Why would I want to teach others?

A: For several reasons. Some people want to teach others because they are in the business of teaching, perhaps in a class in research methods, methodology, needs assessment, or some other subject area, where focus group interviewing is a needed skill. Other researchers want to teach others, but for a very different reason. They want community members (or members of the organization) to own the problem and be committed to finding a solution. If these people are involved in the research study, there is a far greater likelihood that the results will be used. Once people have worked together to obtain information, they develop a common understanding of the problem, and solution strategies are

**For More Details on How to Involve Volunteers and Community Members, See Volume 5,** *Involving Community Members in Focus Groups*

often easier to identify. Still another reason is that others (volunteers) can go places and do things that are impossible for the researcher. Because of the gender, age, race, or background of the researcher, it may be impossible for him or her to moderate the focus groups. In these cases, often the most viable option is to find individuals with the necessary qualifications, teach them focus group skills, and bring them into the research team.

Q: Can I teach focus group interviewing if I haven't conducted focus groups myself?

A: Experience is recommended, but it is optional if you are teaching a class of students in a formal classroom situation. However, if you are working with a team of volunteers in an informal educational environment, then field experience is essential. When working with volunteers, your answers must be practical and efficient. It will be very obvious to the volunteers if you haven't had experience, and then confidence and motivation will decline.

Q: How can I get experience with focus groups?

A: First, volunteer to conduct focus groups in an informal environment. Pick a topic and audience where you personally feel comfortable. It could be for a religious group, civic organization, community club, youth organization, or other group. Keep the focus groups small and discussions short. Second, as your comfort level increases, conduct more focus groups on the topic where you want volunteers to help. (Along the way you're developing stories and experiences that will become valuable teaching examples.) Third, if possible, seek help from a coach. Locate someone who is an expert with focus groups and ask for advice. Fourth, conduct the complete analysis of the focus group and prepare a report that can be used as a model for volunteers. Now you've paid your dues and are ready to share.

Q: Can anyone be a moderator?

A: No. Some people do not have the patience, talent, or personality to moderate focus groups. Attempt to have several ways for volunteers to help. Moderating is only one of the choices. If they are unable to moderate, guide them into other areas.

Q: So what makes for a good moderator?

A: Review the personal qualities of moderators described in Chapter 6 of this volume.

The effective moderator understands group process, is curious, has communication skills, is friendly, has a sense of humor, is interested in people, is open to new ideas, and has superb listening skills. It is interesting that those who should be discouraged from moderating are often those who exude the greatest confidence. These people are the ones who have been successful in public speaking and small group process; they are often called leaders by others. These individuals fail to realize that the key aspects of moderating are these:

**Chapter 6 of This Volume Has a Discussion of the Personal Qualities of Moderators**

- To listen, not to talk
- To understand, not to persuade
- To soak up, not to teach

Q: Do all successful moderators conduct focus groups in the same way?

A: No. Part of moderating is being sincere and genuine. If a moderator tries to act in a way that is not comfortable or familiar, he or she will not do well and will likely be seen as a phony. Don't expect all moderators to be clones of you. Let them be themselves. Allow them some latitude.

Q: So, then, do all moderators just do their own thing?

A: No. This is a research method, and consistency and uniformity are essential in certain things. The selection and recruitment process, the asking of questions, and the analysis process must be consistent and uniform. However, the way moderators give the introduction to the focus group could vary. Sometimes questions are asked in a different order, depending on the interest of the participants. Probes are a judgment call, and although some can be anticipated, many will vary from one group to another.

Q: If only some volunteers are moderators, what do others do?

A: Develop several options for the team members and make assignments based on skills and comfort. Often, we ask for volunteers to serve as moderator, assistant moderator, recruiter, analyst, transcriber, or reporter. Before assignments are made, we have volunteers practice various tasks and then we attempt to match interest and skills.

Q: What are the most important aspects of training?

A: Respect the skills and expertise of volunteers, and teach them in an experiential manner. You've invited the volunteers because they are special. They have contacts, experiences, and background that are essential to the study. Be sure to praise them for their skills. You, as the researcher, bring another set of skills that are also essential. You know how to conceptualize, plan, and conduct the research study in a credible manner. As a researcher, your challenge is to blend both of these needed elements. The second critical aspect is experiential teaching. This means that the teacher demonstrates, uses examples, allows for practice, offers feedback, and then encourages more practice.

Q: I'm a researcher, and I've had no training in working with teams. So, now, do I have to be an expert in teamwork?

A: Increasingly, researchers are being called on to function within the community as teachers, coaches, and mentors. Some researchers are comfortable and capable of making this switch, but others are not. If you feel uncomfortable with this new dimension, you might consider broadening your skills in group dynamics. Another option is to work with someone who is talented at working with groups. This person might coordinate the group, which would enable you to concentrate your attention on the research.

Q: Where can I find out more about teaching a group of volunteers?

A: Read Volume 5 in this series, *Involving Community Members in Focus Groups*.

# References

Andrews, A. (1977, July 11). How to buy productive focus group research. *Advertising Age*, pp. 146-148.

Collier, T. (1996, October). *The secret life of moderators*. Paper presented at the meeting of the Qualitative Research Consultants Association, Montreal, Canada. (Available from Trevor Collier & Co. Ltd., Qualitative Research Consultants, 88 Leuty Ave., Toronto, Ontario M4E 2R4, Canada)

Debus, M. (1986). *Handbook for excellence in focus group research*. Washington, DC: Academy for Education Development.

de Voggelaere, S. (1995, Fall). When the worst happens. *QRCA Views*, p. 25.

Greenbaum, T. L. (1993). *The handbook for focus group research*. New York: Lexington.

Henderson, L., and Perry, B. L. (1994, October). *150 more tips for new moderators*. Paper presented at the meeting of the Qualitative Research Consultants Association, Chicago, IL.

Henderson, N. (1991, December). The art of moderating: A blend of basic skills and qualities. *Quirk's Marketing Research Review*, p. 39.

Kelleher, J. (1982). Find out what your customers really want. *Inc. 4*(1), 88, 91.

Kornfield, J. (1993). *A path with heart*. New York: Bantam.

Langer, J. (1978, September 21). Clients: Check qualitative researcher's personal traits to get more. Qualitative researchers: Enter entire marketing process to give more. *Marketing News*, pp. 10-11.

Langer, J. (1991, December). How to keep respondents from taking over focus groups. *Quirk's Marketing Research Review*, pp. 34-38.

Mariampolski, H. (1991, December). *Quirk's Marketing Research Review*, p. 42.

Perry, B. L. (1994, October). *150 more tips for new moderators.* Paper presented at the meeting of the Qualitative Research Consultants Association, Chicago, IL.

# Index to This Volume

# Index to the Focus Group Kit

The letter preceding the page number refers to the volume, according to the following key:

G   Volume 1:   *The Focus Group Guidebook*
P   Volume 2:   *Planning Focus Groups*
Q   Volume 3:   *Developing Questions for Focus Groups*
M   Volume 4:   *Moderating Focus Groups*
I   Volume 5:   *Involving Community Members in Focus Groups*
A   Volume 6:   *Analyzing and Reporting Focus Group Results*

# About the Author

Richard A. Krueger is a professor and evaluation leader at the University of Minnesota. He teaches in the College of Education and Human Development and serves as an evaluation specialist with the University of Minnesota Extension Service. Over the past decade, he has taught hundreds of people to plan, conduct, and analyze focus group interviews. He loves stories. Perhaps that is what drew him to focus group inter-
views. Where else can one hear so many stories in such a short period of time?